Learning Jupyter

Learn how to write code, mathematics, graphics, and output, all in a single document, as well as in a web browser using Project Jupyter

Dan Toomey

BIRMINGHAM - MUMBAI

Learning Jupyter

First published: November 2016

Production reference: 1241116

Published by Packt Publishing Ltd.
Livery Place
35 Livery Street
Birmingham
B3 2PB, UK.
ISBN 978-1-78588-487-0

www.packtpub.com

Credits

Author

Dan Toomey

Copy Editors

Vikrant Phadke
Safis Editing

Reviewer

Jesse Bacon

Project Coordinator

Nidhi Joshi

Commissioning Editor

Veena Pagare

Proofreader

Safis Editing

Acquisition Editor

Manish Nainani

Indexer

Mariammal Chettiyar

Content Development Editor

Aishwarya Pandere

Graphics

Disha Haria

Technical Editor

Prasad Ramesh

Production Coordinator

Nilesh Mohite

About the Author

Dan Toomey has been developing applications for over 20 years. He has worked in a variety of industries and size companies in roles from sole contributor to VP/CTO level. For the last 10 years or so, he has been contracting to companies in the eastern Massachusetts area. Dan has been contracting under Dan Toomey Software Corp. Again, as a contractor developer in the area. Dan has also written *R for Data Sciences* with Packt Publishing.

About the Reviewer

Jesse Bacon is a hobbyist programmer and technologist in the Washington D.C. metro area. In his free time, he mostly works through a new title about an interesting technology or spends time at the gym. Mr. Bacon values the opinions of the development community and looks forward to a new generation of programmers with all the gifts of today's computing environments.

www.PacktPub.com

For support files and downloads related to your book, please visit www.PacktPub.com.

Did you know that Packt offers eBook versions of every book published, with PDF and ePub files available? You can upgrade to the eBook version at www.PacktPub.com and as a print book customer, you are entitled to a discount on the eBook copy. Get in touch with us at service@packtpub.com for more details.

At www.PacktPub.com, you can also read a collection of free technical articles, sign up for a range of free newsletters and receive exclusive discounts and offers on Packt books and eBooks.

https://www.packtpub.com/mapt

Get the most in-demand software skills with Mapt. Mapt gives you full access to all Packt books and video courses, as well as industry-leading tools to help you plan your personal development and advance your career.

Why subscribe?

- Fully searchable across every book published by Packt
- Copy and paste, print, and bookmark content
- On demand and accessible via a web browser

Table of Contents

Preface

Learning Jupyter discusses using Jupyter to record your scripts and results for a data analysis project. Jupyter allows the data scientist to record their complete analysis process, much in the same way other scientists use a lab notebook for recording tests, progress, results and conclusions. Jupyter works in a variety of operating systems and the book covers the use of Jupyter in Windows and Mac OS X along with the various steps necessary to enable your specific needs. Jupyter supports a variety of scripting languages by the addition of language engines so the user can portray their script natively in it.

What this book covers

Chapter 1, *Introduction to Jupyter*, takes a first look at the Jupyter user interface, walks through installing Jupyter on Windows and Mac OS X, examines the basic operations of Jupyter Notebook available through the user interface for all engines, and gives an overview of the security features available and configuration options.

Chapter 2, *Jupyter Python Scripting*, walks through a simple Python notebook and the underlying structure. This chapter also shows an example of using pandas, graphics, and using random numbers in a Python script.

Chapter 3, *Jupyter R Scripting*, adds the ability to use R scripts in your Jupyter Notebook, adds an R library not included in the standard R installation, makes a Hello World script in R, and shows R data access against built-in libraries and some of the simpler graphics and statistics that are automatically generated. We use an R script to generate 3D graphics in a couple of different ways, perform a cluster analysis, and use one of the forecasting tools available in R.

Chapter 4, *Jupyter Julia Scripting*, adds the ability to use Julia scripts in your Jupyter Notebook, adds a Julia library not included in the standard Julia installation, and shows the basic features of Julia. We outline some of the limitations encountered with using Julia in Jupyter and display graphics using some of the graphics packages available, including Gadfly, Winston, Vega, and Pyplot. We show parallel processing in action, a small control flow example, and how to add unit testing to your Julia script.

Chapter 5, *Jupyter JavaScript Coding*, shows how to add JavaScript to a Jupyter Notebook, some of the limitations of using Javascript in Jupyter and examples of several packages that are exemplary of Node.js coding, including d3 for graphics, stats-analysis for statistics, built-in JSON handling, Canvas for creating graphics files and Plotly used for generating graphics with a third-party tool. You learn how multi-threaded applications can be developed using Node.js under Jupyter and use machine learning to develop a decision tree.

Chapter 6, *Interactive Widgets, adds widgets to our Jupyter installation*, uses interact and interactive widgets to produce a variety of user input controls. We explain the widgets package in depth to investigate the user controls available, properties available in the containers, and events that are available emitting from the controls. You will see how to build containers of controls.

Chapter 7, *Sharing and Converting Jupyter Notebooks*, shares notebooks on a notebook server, adds a notebook to a web server, distributes at notebook using GitHub, and looks into converting our notebooks into different formats, such as HTML and PDF.

Chapter 8, *Multiuser Jupyter Notebooks*, exposes a notebook so that multiple users can use a notebook at the same time, and shows an example of the multiuser *error* occurring. We will install a Jupyter server that overcomes the multiuser issue and use Docker to alleviate the issue as well.

Chapter 9, *Jupyter Scala*, installs Scala for Jupyter, uses Scala coding to access larger datasets, shows how Scala can manipulate arrays, and generates random numbers in Scala. There are examples of higher-order functions and pattern matching, uses case classes, and immutability in Scala. We build collections using Scala packages and show the use of Scala traits.

Chapter 10, *Jupyter and Big Data*, uses Spark functionality via Python coding for Jupyter, installs the Spark additions to Jupyter on a Windows machine and a Mac machine, and displays an initial script that just reads lines from a text file. We also determine the word counts in that file, sort the results, use a script to estimate pi, evaluate web log files for anomalies, determine a set of prime numbers, and evaluate a text stream for some characteristics.

What you need for this book

The steps in this book assume you have a modern Windows or Macintosh machine with Internet access. There are several points where you will need to install software, so you need administrative privileges to the machine to do so.

Who this book is for

This book is written for the user who wants to portray software to others in a natural programming context. Jupyter provides the mechanism to execute a number of different languages and stores the results for display as if the user ran those scripts on their machine.

Conventions

In this book, you will find a number of text styles that distinguish between different kinds of information. Here are some examples of these styles and an explanation of their meaning.

Code words in text, database table names, folder names, filenames, file extensions, pathnames, dummy URLs, user input, and Twitter handles are shown as follows: "Interestingly, the max function does not work as expected."

A block of code is set as follows:

```
{
  "cells": [
    <<same format as seen earlier for the cells>>
  ],
  "metadata": {
    "kernelspec": {
      "display_name": "Javascript (Node.js)",
      "language": "javascript",
      "name": "javascript"
    },
    "language_info": {
      "file_extension": ".js",
      "mimetype": "application/javascript",
      "name": "javascript",
      "version": "4.2.4"
    }
  },
  "nbformat": 4,
  "nbformat_minor": 0
}
```

Any command-line input or output is written as follows:

```
Pkg.add("DataFrames")
Pkg.add("RDatasets")
Pkg.add("Gadfly")
quit();
```

New terms and **important words** are shown in bold. Words that you see on the screen, for example, in menus or dialog boxes, appear in the text like this: "The **Upload** button is used to add files to the notebook space."

Warnings or important notes appear in a box like this.

Tips and tricks appear like this.

Reader feedback

Feedback from our readers is always welcome. Let us know what you think about this book-what you liked or disliked. Reader feedback is important for us as it helps us develop titles that you will really get the most out of. To send us general feedback, simply e-mail feedback@packtpub.com, and mention the book's title in the subject of your message. If there is a topic that you have expertise in and you are interested in either writing or contributing to a book, see our author guide at www.packtpub.com/authors.

Customer support

Now that you are the proud owner of a Packt book, we have a number of things to help you to get the most from your purchase.

Downloading the example code

You can download the example code files for this book from your account at http://www.packtpub.com. If you purchased this book elsewhere, you can visit http://www.packtpub.com/support and register to have the files e-mailed directly to you.

You can download the code files by following these steps:

1. Log in or register to our website using your e-mail address and password.
2. Hover the mouse pointer on the **SUPPORT** tab at the top.
3. Click on **Code Downloads & Errata**.
4. Enter the name of the book in the **Search** box.
5. Select the book for which you're looking to download the code files.
6. Choose from the drop-down menu where you purchased this book from.
7. Click on **Code Download**.

Once the file is downloaded, please make sure that you unzip or extract the folder using the latest version of:

- WinRAR / 7-Zip for Windows
- Zipeg / iZip / UnRarX for Mac
- 7-Zip / PeaZip for Linux

The code bundle for the book is also hosted on GitHub at `https://github.com/PacktPublishing/Learning-Jupyter`. We also have other code bundles from our rich catalog of books and videos available at `https://github.com/PacktPublishing/`. Check them out!

Downloading the color images of this book

We also provide you with a PDF file that has color images of the screenshots/diagrams used in this book. The color images will help you better understand the changes in the output. You can download this file from `https://www.packtpub.com/sites/default/files/downloads/LearningJupyter_ColorImages.pdf`.

Errata

Although we have taken every care to ensure the accuracy of our content, mistakes do happen. If you find a mistake in one of our books-maybe a mistake in the text or the code-we would be grateful if you could report this to us. By doing so, you can save other readers from frustration and help us improve subsequent versions of this book. If you find any errata, please report them by visiting `http://www.packtpub.com/submit-errata`, selecting your book, clicking on the **Errata Submission Form** link, and entering the details of your errata. Once your errata are verified, your submission will be accepted and the errata will be uploaded to our website or added to any list of existing errata under the Errata section of that title.

To view the previously submitted errata, go to https://www.packtpub.com/books/content/support and enter the name of the book in the search field. The required information will appear under the **Errata** section.

Piracy

Piracy of copyrighted material on the Internet is an ongoing problem across all media. At Packt, we take the protection of our copyright and licenses very seriously. If you come across any illegal copies of our works in any form on the Internet, please provide us with the location address or website name immediately so that we can pursue a remedy.

Please contact us at copyright@packtpub.com with a link to the suspected pirated material.

We appreciate your help in protecting our authors and our ability to bring you valuable content.

Questions

If you have a problem with any aspect of this book, you can contact us at questions@packtpub.com, and we will do our best to address the problem.

1
Introduction to Jupyter

Jupyter is a tool that allows data scientists to record their complete analysis process, much in the same way other scientists use a lab notebook to record tests, progress, results, and conclusions.

The Jupyter product was originally developed as part of the **IPython** project. The IPython project was used to provide interactive online access to Python. Over time it became useful to interact with other data analysis tools, such as R, in the same manner. With this split from Python, the tool grew into its current manifestation of Jupyter. IPython is still an active tool that's available for use. The name Jupyter itself is derived from the combination of Julia, Python, and R.

Jupyter is available as a web application from a number of places. It can also be used locally over a wide variety of installations. In this book, we will be exploring using Jupyter on a Mac and a Windows PC and over the Internet with other providers.

In this chapter, we will cover the following topics:

- First look at Jupyter
- Installing Jupyter on Windows
- Installing Jupyter on Mac
- Notebook structure
- Notebook workflow
- Basic notebook operations
- Security in Jupyter
- Configuration options for Jupyter

First look at Jupyter

Here is a sample opening page when using Jupyter (this screenshot is on a Windows machine):

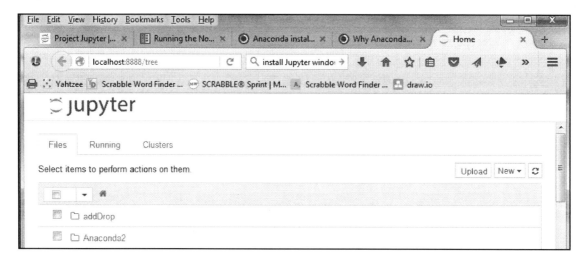

You should get yourself acquainted with the environment. The Jupyter user interface has a number of components:

- Product title, **Jupyter**, in the top left (as expected). The logo and the title name are clickable and will return you to the Jupyter Notebook home page.
- There are three tabs displayed: **Files**, **Running**, and **Clusters**:

- The **Files** tab shows the list of files in the current directory of the page (described later on in this section).
- The **Running** tab presents another screen of the currently running processes and notebooks. The drop-down lists for **Terminals** and **Notebooks** are populated with their running members:

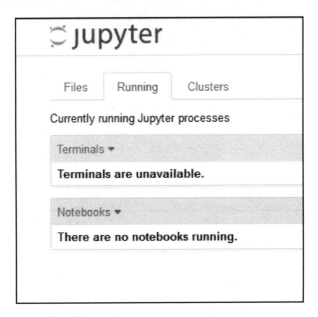

- The **Clusters** tab presents another screen to display the list of clusters available. This topic is covered in a later chapter:

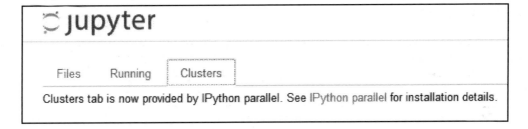

- In the top right corner of the screen are three buttons: **Upload**, **New** (menu), and a Refresh button.
- The **Upload** button is used to add files to the notebook space. You may also just drag and drop as you would when handling files. Similarly, you can drag and drop notebooks into specific folders as well.

- The menu with **New** at the top presents a further menu of **Text File**, **Folder**, **Terminals Unavailable**, **Notebooks**, and **Python 2**:

- The **Text File** option is used to add a text file to the current directory. Jupyter will open a new browser window for you running a text editor. The text entered is automatically saved and will be displayed in your notebook's **Files** display:

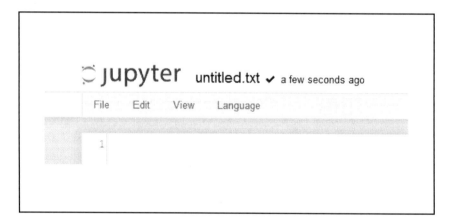

 The default filename, `untitled.txt`, is editable.

- The **Folder** option creates a new folder with the name `Untitled Folder`. Remember, all of the file/folder names are editable:

- The **Terminals Unavailable** option is disabled for Windows. On a Mac, the option allows you to start an IPython session.
- The **Notebooks** option will be activated when additional notebooks are available in your environment.
- The **Python 2** option is used to begin a **Python 2** session interactively in your notebook. The interface looks like the following screenshot. You have full file editing capabilities for your script, including saving as a new file. You also have a complete working IDE for your Python script:

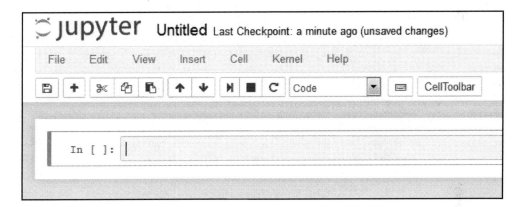

Like the **Text File** and **Folder** option, you have created a Python script file in your notebook and it is running!

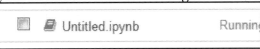

- The refresh button is used to update the display. It's not really necessary as the display is reactive to any changes in the underlying file structure.
- At the top of the **Files** tab's item list is a checkbox, a drop-down menu, and a home button:
    - The checkbox is used to toggle all the checkboxes in the Items list
    - The drop-down menu presents a list of the choices available, **Folders**, **All Notebooks**, **Running**, and **Files**, as shown in the following screenshot:

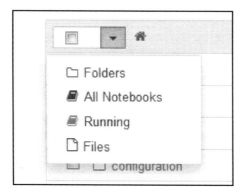

- The **Folders** selection will select all the folders in the display and present a count of the folders in the small box
- The **All Notebooks** selection will change the count to the number of notebooks and provide you with three options:
    - Duplicate the current notebook
    - Shut down the current notebook
    - Trash the current notebook

- You can see them in the following screenshot:

- The **Running** selection will select any running scripts and update the count to the number selected

- The **Files** selection will select all of the files in the notebook display and update the count accordingly
- The home button brings you back to the home screen of the notebook.

On the left-hand side of every item is a checkbox, an icon, and the item's name:

- The checkbox is used to build a set of files to operate upon.
- The icon is indicative of the type of item. In this case, all of the items are folders.
- The name of the item corresponds to the name of the object. In this case, the filenames are as used on the disk.

Installing Jupyter on Windows

Jupyter requires Python to be installed (it is based on the Python language). There are a couple of tools that will automate the installation of Jupyter (and optionally Python) from a GUI. In this case, we are showing how to install using **Anaconda**, which is a Python tool for distributing software. You first have to install Anaconda. It is available on Windows and Mac environments. Download the executable from `https://www.continuum.io/` (company that produces Anaconda) and run it to install Anaconda. The software provides a regular installation setup process, as shown in the following screenshot:

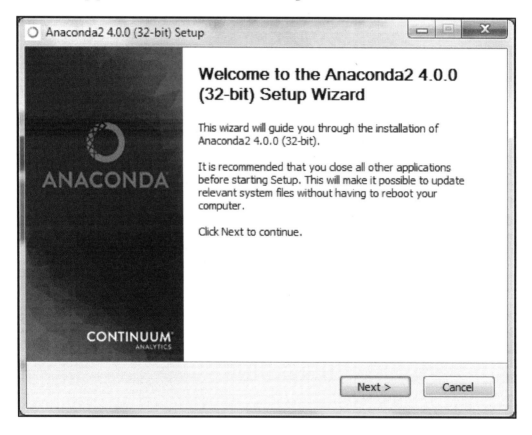

The installation process goes through the regular steps of making you agree to the distribution rights license:

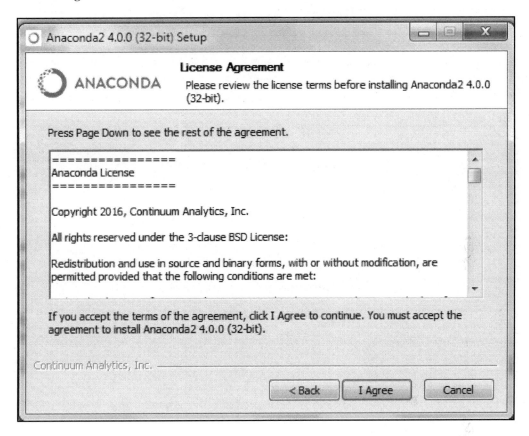

The standard Windows installation allows you to decide whether all users on the machine can run the new software or not. If you are sharing a machine with different levels of users, then you can decide the appropriate action:

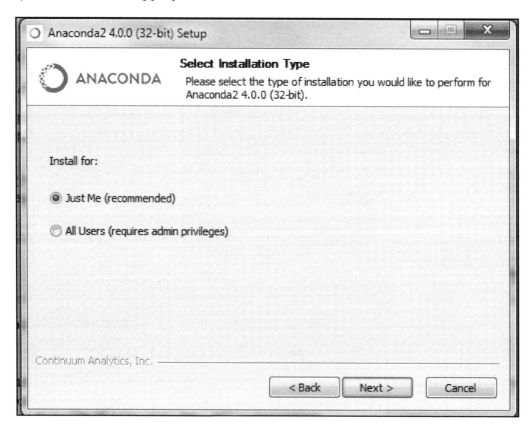

After clicking on **Next**, it will ask for a destination for the software to reside (I almost always keep the default paths):

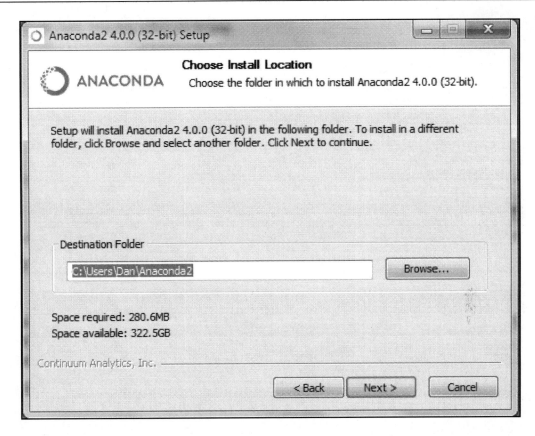

And, most importantly, make sure that Python installed with Anaconda provides your Python basis going forward (by being placed in the execution path). Remember, Anaconda uses Python tool itself, so this is important.

 This process takes some time to download and install.

Once Anaconda is installed, you need to run a command-line instruction to install Jupyter. The command is as follows:

```
conda install jupyter
```

This will invoke a process to download all the necessary components for Jupyter onto your PC. Your output should look something like this:

```
C:\Users\Dan>conda install jupyter
Using Anaconda Cloud api site https://api.anaconda.org
Fetching package metadata: ....
Solving package specifications: ........
# packages in environment at C:\Users\Dan\Anaconda2:
#
jupyter                     1.0.0                    py27_2
```

 Additional lines will be present for an install. I have abbreviated the output. You now have Jupyter installed on your machine. You can start the process using the following command:

```
C:\Users\Dan>jupyter notebook
```

This command is starting a Jupyter Notebook server on your machine. Once the server is started, a browser instance will be opened at the starting point of the notebook. You should see logging statements similar to the following on your machine as the server starts:

```
    [I 16:21:59.144 NotebookApp] Writing notebook server cookie secret to
C:\Users\Dan\AppData\Roaming\jupyter\runtime\notebook_cookie_secret
    [I 16:21:59.846 NotebookApp] Serving notebooks from local directory:
C:\Users\Dan
    [I 16:21:59.846 NotebookApp] 0 active kernels
    [I 16:21:59.846 NotebookApp] The Jupyter Notebook is running at:
http://localhost:8888/
    [I 16:21:59.862 NotebookApp] Use Control-C to stop this server and shut
down all kernels (twice to skip confirmation).
```

Once Jupyter is running, you will notice a running icon for Jupyter (two inverted crescents) at the bottom of your screen:

Note, the last line of the log is the instruction you must use to stop the server (press *Ctrl* + *C* in the command-line window where the server is running).

If you press *Ctrl* + *C* in that window, the Jupyter server will shut down gracefully:

```
    [W 17:26:36.688 NotebookApp] 404 GET /favicon.ico (::1) 62.00ms
referer=None
    [W 17:26:36.750 NotebookApp] 404 GET /favicon.ico (::1) 0.00ms
referer=None
    [I 17:28:24.891 NotebookApp] Interrupted...
    [I 17:28:24.891 NotebookApp] Shutting down kernels
```

You will notice that the Anaconda package has been installed on your application menu for further use:

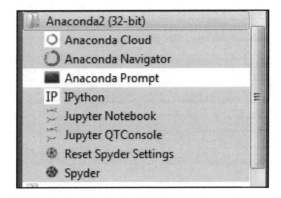

Installing Jupyter on Mac

On Mac, you can use the same Anaconda GUI (for Mac) as described in the previous section. You may also use the command-line tools available for Linux on your Mac.

You must first install Anaconda. Download the latest version and execute the embedded shell script to install.

Installing Jupyter on Mac is done through the command line using the `conda install` command:

```
bmac:~ dtoomey$ conda install jupyter
Fetching package metadata: ....
Solving package specifications: ...................................
Package plan for installation in environment /Users/dtoomey/anaconda:
```

The following packages will be downloaded:

```
    package                    |              build
    ---------------------------|-----------------
    mistune-0.7.2              |           py27_1         178 KB
    setuptools-20.3            |           py27_0         453 KB
    conda-4.0.5               |           py27_0         185 KB
    pexpect-4.0.1             |           py27_0          63 KB
    traitlets-4.2.1           |           py27_0         108 KB
    ipython-4.1.2             |           py27_2         931 KB
    jupyter_core-4.1.0        |           py27_0          51 KB
    jupyter_client-4.2.2      |           py27_0          96 KB
    jupyter_console-4.1.1     |           py27_0          24 KB
    notebook-4.1.0            |           py27_2         4.4 MB
    qtconsole-4.2.1           |           py27_0         160 KB
    jupyter-1.0.0             |           py27_2           2 KB
    ------------------------------------------------------------
                                           Total:         6.6 MB
```

The following packages will be updated:

```
    conda:           3.19.3-py27_0 --> 4.0.5-py27_0
    ipython:         4.1.2-py27_0  --> 4.1.2-py27_2
    jupyter:         1.0.0-py27_1  --> 1.0.0-py27_2
    jupyter_client:  4.1.1-py27_0  --> 4.2.2-py27_0
    jupyter_console: 4.1.0-py27_0  --> 4.1.1-py27_0
    jupyter_core:    4.0.6-py27_0  --> 4.1.0-py27_0
    mistune:         0.7.1-py27_0  --> 0.7.2-py27_1
    notebook:        4.1.0-py27_0  --> 4.1.0-py27_2
    pexpect:         3.3-py27_0    --> 4.0.1-py27_0
    qtconsole:       4.1.1-py27_0  --> 4.2.1-py27_0
    setuptools:      20.1.1-py27_0 --> 20.3-py27_0
    traitlets:       4.1.0-py27_0  --> 4.2.1-py27_0
Proceed ([y]/n)? y
Fetching packages ...
mistune-0.7.2- 100% |################| Time: 0:00:00   1.87 MB/s
setuptools-20. 100% |################| Time: 0:00:00   3.53 MB/s
conda-4.0.5-py 100% |################| Time: 0:00:00   2.47 MB/s
pexpect-4.0.1- 100% |################| Time: 0:00:00   1.26 MB/s
traitlets-4.2. 100% |################| Time: 0:00:00   1.71 MB/s
```

```
ipython-4.1.2-  100%  |################|  Time:  0:00:00   1.77 MB/s
jupyter_core-4  100%  |################|  Time:  0:00:00   2.34 MB/s
jupyter_client  100%  |################|  Time:  0:00:00   1.58 MB/s
jupyter_consol  100%  |################|  Time:  0:00:00   7.82 MB/s
notebook-4.1.0  100%  |################|  Time:  0:00:00   4.75 MB/s
qtconsole-4.2.  100%  |################|  Time:  0:00:00   1.37 MB/s
jupyter-1.0.0-  100%  |################|  Time:  0:00:00   2.71 MB/s
Extracting packages ...
[        COMPLETE ]|#########################################| 100%
Unlinking packages ...
[        COMPLETE ]|#########################################| 100%
Linking packages ...
[        COMPLETE ]|#########################################| 100%
```

You have installed Jupyter.

Notebook structure

A Jupyter Notebook is fundamentally a JSON file with a number of annotations. The main parts of the Notebook are as follows:

- **Metadata**: A data dictionary of definitions used to set up and display the notebook
- **Notebook format**: Version numbers of the software used to create the notebook (the version number is used for backward compatibility)
- **List of cells**: There are different types of cell for markdown (display), code (to execute), and output (of the code type cells)

Notebook workflow

The typical workflow is as follows:

- Create a new notebook for a project or data analysis.
- Add your analysis steps, coding, and output.

- Surround your analysis with organizational and presentation markdown to communicate an entire story.
- Interactive notebooks (that include widgets and display modules) would then be used by others by modifying parameters and data to note the effects of their changes. Your markdown would present the cases that a user may want to investigate and probable results.

Basic notebook operations

In this section, we describe the different operations that you can perform on your Jupyter Notebook. Most of the operations are menu functions that will change your display accordingly.

File operations

Let's walk through the basic file operations.

From the **Files** tab, we see a list of files and folders in the current notebook/disk folder. If we select (check) one of the files, we see the top-left menu change:

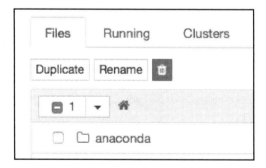

We now have choices of **Duplicate**, **Rename**, and delete (the trashcan icon). Note the number of files selected, **1**, is displayed in the box as well.

Duplicate

If we hit the **Duplicate** button, we get a confirmation prompt with the name of the file selected for duplication:

Cancel will close the dialog. **Duplicate** will create another copy of the file with an appended copy number, as in the following screenshot. The original filename has been used with the addition of -Copyn in the filename, where n is the copy number. Note the original file extension, .properties, has been maintained in the new file:

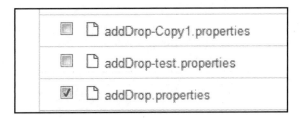

Rename

Similarly, if we hit the **Rename** button, another dialog box will appear to prompt the new filename to apply. The main filename has been highlighted as it assumes you want to maintain the file extension as the file type has not changed:

Delete

We can also delete the file by clicking on the trashcan icon. This brings up a confirmation dialog box:

At the top right of the screen we have options for **Upload** and **New** (**Text File**, **Folder**, or **Python 2**).

Upload

The **Upload** button is more meaningful when the notebook is stored on a web server. When running it on your desktop, it allows you to move files easily from one part of your notebook to another. If you click the button, you are presented with a file selector dialog box. The following screenshot is specific to a Windows environment, but a similar display is presented on a Mac. Once you select a file, it will be added to your notebook space:

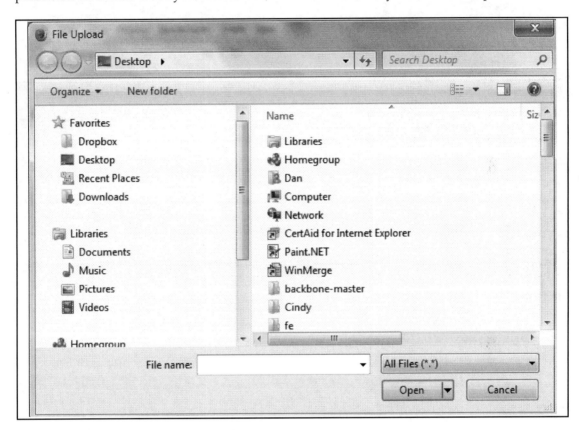

New text file

If we opt to create a **New Text File**, we are presented with a new browser panel in the Jupyter text editor (Note that I have shrunk down the size of the screen so the display fits the boundaries of this book):

There are several points of interest on this screen:

- We are in a new browser panel (the notebook display is still present in the other tab).
- The name of the new file is untitled1.txt. Using the same convention as duplication, the new filename starts with untitled.txt and is incremented as needed.
- Curiously, it mentions when the file was created.
- In the top-right corner, we see **Plain Text**. So, we might expect to see some other description here for other file types.
- We have a new menu, **File**, **Edit**, **View**, and **Language**.

- The **File** menu has the following options:
    - **New**: Start another new text window
    - **Save**: Save/update the current text file into the notebook area

- **Rename**: Change the name of the file (unlikely you would want to keep the `untitledn` name provided)
- **Download**: Again, an option that makes more sense if your notebook is running on the Web. As explained for **Upload**, **Download** on a desktop installation allows you to copy a file to another part of your machine.

- The **Edit** menu has the following options:
  - **Find**: Search for a string.
  - **Find & Replace**: Search for and replace a string.
  - **Separator**: The options for adjusting the text editor in use are below this line.
  - **Key Map**: Set your own function mapping for your keyboard.
  - **Default**: Checked as it is the default choice. This means to use the default text editor.
  - **Sublime text**: If you would prefer to use the Sublime editor.
  - **Vim**: If you would prefer to use Vim.
  - **Emacs**: If you would prefer to use Emacs.

- The **View** menu only has an option to **Toggle Line Numbers**. I imagine future revisions of the package will have additional features. Similarly, for other file types, the menu may change.
- The **Language** menu allows you to specify whether this text file is a specific type of programming file. This allows syntax highlighting, which is a major feature of source editors. The list is extensive:

New folder

The **New Folder** option creates a new folder with the naming convention `Untitled Folder n`.

New Python 2

The **New Python 2** option creates a new Python 2 session. You are presented with a new browser panel with a similar naming convention, as seen in the following screenshot.

This is a very different presentation, where Python code is expected to be entered in the cells on the page with results displayed below each cell.

There is an extensive menu with **File**, **Edit**, **View**, **Insert**, **Cell**, **Kernel**, and **Help** options. We have a fairly complete **Integrated Development Environment** (**IDE**) for creating Python coding:

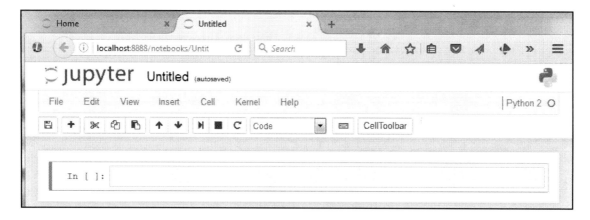

The **File** menu has the following options:

- **New Notebook**: Start a new notebook (another browser panel like this one)
- **Open…**: Select a file to open from the notebook **Files** view
- **Make a Copy…**: Copy the current notebook completely into another browser panel
- **Rename…**: Rename the current notebook
- **Save and Checkpoint**: Save the current notebook and record a checkpoint

A checkpoint is a point in time where all information about a notebook is preserved. You can have many checkpoints and return the state of your notebook to the previous checkpoint state at any time. This is an excellent way to give yourself the room to try out a new angle on your analysis without risking losing what you have done so far.

- **Revert to Checkpoint**: Revert your notebook to a previous checkpoint
- **Print Preview**: Present a preview of the printed form of your notebook
- **Download as**: Download the notebook in a variety of formats:
    - IPython notebook (its current form)
    - IPython
    - HTML representation
    - Markdown–a specialized display format
    - reST–**reStructuredText**–an easy to read, plain text markup
    - PDF
    - Presentation
- **Close and Halt**: Close the current notebook and stop any running scripts

The **Edit** menu has the following options:

- **Cut Cells**: Cut the currently selected cells to the clipboard

 Each of the rectangular work areas in your notebook is a cell. The innermost text area is where you enter code. Below that (but within the surrounding rectangle), the results of each code stop will be displayed.

- **Copy Cells**: Copy cells from the clipboard to the current cursor position
- **Paste Cells Above**: Paste cells from the clipboard above the current cell
- **Paste Cells Below**: Paste cells from the clipboard below the current cell
- **Paste Cells & Replace**: Paste the cells from the clipboard on top of the current cell
- **Delete Cells**: Delete the current cells
- **Undo Delete Cells**: Revert the last Delete Cells invocation
- **Split Cell**: Split up a cell from the current cursor position
- **Merge Cell Above**: Merge the current cell with the one above

- **Merge Cell Below**: Merge the current cell with the one below
- **Edit Notebook Metadata**: Every notebook has underlying **metadata** that describes the characteristics of the notebook. Advanced users can manipulate this data directly in order to adjust features more readily. For example, the current notebook metadata looks like the following screenshot:

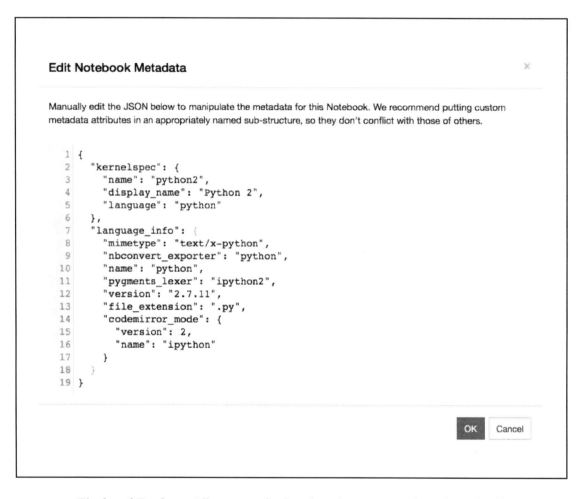

- **Find and Replace**: Allow us to find and replace among the selected cells. There is a standardized dialog box for this, as shown in the following screenshot:

As seen in the preceding screenshot, the parameters and their functions are as follows:

- The **Aa** icon toggle determines whether a case-insensitive search is made
- The * icon toggle determines whether a regex search is made
- The stacked lines icon toggle is whether a replace will be made
- The **Find** text block presents the search criteria
- The **Replace** text block is used for the replacement text

The **View** menu has the following options:

- **Toggle Header**: Toggles the display of the Jupyter logo and filename
- **Toggle Toolbar**: Toggles the display of the toolbar
- **Cell Toolbar**: Toggles the display of the cell action icons

The **Insert** menu has the following options:

- **Insert Cell Above**: Add a new cell above the current one
- **Insert Cell Below**: Add a new cell below the current one

The **Cell** menu has the following options:

- **Run Cells**: Run the selected (or all) cells.
- **Run Cells and Select Below**: Run the current cells down and create a new one below.
- **Run Cells and Insert Below**: Run the current cells and create a new one above.
- **Run All**: Run all cells.
- **Run All Above**: Run all cells prior to the current cell.

- **Run All Below**: Run all cells below the current cell.
- **Cell Type**: Change the type of cell selected to **Code**, **Markdown**, or **Raw NBConvert**. There is an automatic message that is displayed noting that all cells are by default Code type.
- **Current Outputs and All Output** have options to toggle their display.

The **Kernel** menu has the following options:

- **Interrupt**: Send a keyboard interrupt, *Ctrl + C*, to the kernel. This is useful if your code is in an endless loop.
- **Restart**: Restart the kernel.
- **Restart & Clear Output**: Restart the kernel and clear all output anew.
- **Restart & Run All**: Restart the kernel and run all cells.
- **Reconnect**: Connect back to a remote notebook.
- **Change Kernel**: Not useful as only **Python 2** is available at this point.

The **Help** menu has the following options:

- **User Interface Tour**: Walk the user through a UI tour
- **Keyboard Shortcuts**: Presents a list of built-in keyboard shortcuts
- **Notebook Help**: Help topics on the notebook
- **Markdown**: Description of the markdown available within a notebook
- **Python, IPython, NumPy, SciPy, Matplotlib, SymPy, Pandas**: Help topics on the various languages and packages that can be used in notebooks
- **About**: A standard about box

There is an icon panel below the menu that has shortcut icons for the following functions:

- **Floppy disk icon**: Save and Checkpoint
- **Plus sign**: Insert Cell Below
- **Scissors**: Cut Cell
- **Duplicate pages**: Copy Cell
- **Up arrow**: Move Cell Up
- **Down arrow**: Move Cell Down
- **An icon that looks like a speaker**: Run the current cell
- **Black square**: Interrupt Kernel

- **Circular arrow:** Restart the Kernel

- There's a drop-down menu for display characteristics:
  - **Code**
  - **Markdown**
  - **Raw NBConvert**
  - **Heading**

- **Keyboard:** Open the command palette
- Change the current toolbar in use. Clicking on the **Cell Toolbar** button auto-displays the **Cell Toolbar** choice from the **View** menu:

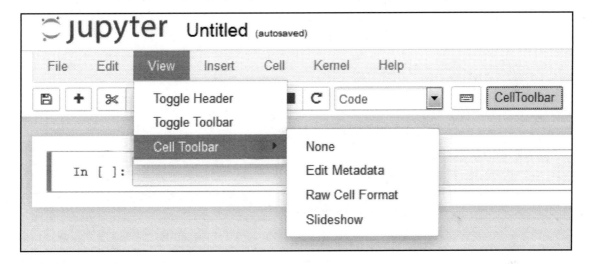

Security in Jupyter

Jupyter notebooks are created in order to be shared with other users, in many cases over the Internet. However, Jupyter notebooks can execute arbitrary code and generate arbitrary code. This can be a problem if malicious aspects have been placed in a notebook. The default security mechanisms for Jupyter notebooks include the following:

- Raw HTML is always sanitized (checked for malicious coding). Further information can be found at `https://developers.google.com/caja`.
- You cannot run external JavaScript.

- Cell contents (especially HTML and JavaScript) are not trusted (requires user validation to continue).
- The output from any cell is not trusted.
- All other HTML or JavaScript is never trusted. Clearing the output will cause the notebook to become trusted when saved.

Security digest

Notebooks can also use a security digest to ensure the correct user is modifying the contents. A digest takes into account the entire contents of the notebook and a secret (only known by the notebook creator). This combination ensures that malicious coding is not going to be added to a notebook.

You add a security digest to a notebook using the following command:

```
~/.jupyter/profile_default/security/notebook_secret
```

Here, you replace the notebook_secret part with your secret.

Trust options

You can specifically apply your trust to a notebook using a command-line option:

```
jupyter trust /path/to/notebook.ipynb
```

Or you can do it once the notebook is opened by the **File** | **Trusted Notebook** menu option.

Configuration options for Jupyter

You can configure some of the display parameters used when presenting notebooks. These are configurable due to the use of a product (CodeMirror) to present and modify the notebook. CodeMirror is a JavaScript-based editor for use within web pages (notebooks).

The list of configurable options is still in development. Some of the options are as follows:

- lineSeparator: The character used to separate text lines
- theme: The overall theme of presentation used in the notebook
- indentUnit: How many spaces to indent blocks of coding

To change the configuration of one of the options, you open the JavaScript window of your browser, enter the coding to modify an option, and then load your notebook. Then the modifications you made would be applied to the notebook presentation. There is further documentation available at `https://codemirror.net/doc/manual.html#option_indentU nit`.

For example, to change the indentation (indent-unit) for your notebook, you would use the following JavaScript:

```
var mycell = Jupyter.notebook.get_selected_cell();
var cell_config = mycell.config;
var code_patch = {
    CodeCell:{
      cm_config:{indentUnit:2}
    }
  }
cell_config.update(code_patch)
```

You have now seen all of the standard operations available to you in a Jupyter Notebook.

Summary

In this chapter, we investigated the various user interface elements available in a notebook. We learned how to install the software on a Mac or a PC. We were exposed to the notebook structure. We saw the typical workflow used when developing a notebook. We walked through the user interface operations available in a notebook. And lastly, we saw some of the configuration options available to advanced users for their notebook.

In the next chapter, we will learn all about Python scripting in a Jupyter Notebook.

2
Jupyter Python Scripting

Jupyter was originally IPython–an interactive version of Python to be used as a development environment. As such, most of the features of Python are available to you when developing your notebook.

In this chapter, we will cover the following topics:

- Basic Python scripting
- Python dataset access (from a library)
- Python pandas
- Python graphics
- Python random numbers

Basic Python in Jupyter

In this chapter, we will be using Python scripts in a Jupyter Notebook. Jupyter does not interact with your scripts as much as it executes your script and records results. I think this is how Jupyter Notebooks have been extended to use other languages besides Python–the notebook just takes a script, runs it against a language engine, and records the output from the engine–all the while not really knowing what kind of script is being executed.

Similarly, I have not noticed any particular limitations when using Python in Jupyter. Some of the scripts I have run have taken a lot of time to run, used a lot of memory, opened new windows, and so on, all without failing. There are known issues running Python scripts that contain a __main__ execution loop and multithreaded applications.

We must open a Python section to our notebook to use Python coding. So, start your notebook, then, in the upper-right menu, select **Python 2**.

I installed Jupyter in the Spring of 2016 on a Windows machine and on a Mac. They both show the menu choice for **Python 2**. I know that elsewhere, requirements talk about later versions of Python being a requirement, but the installed version with Jupyter was 2. (Actually, in the metadata displays, it was 2.7)

The menu is shown in the following screenshot:

This will open a Python window to work in, as shown in the following screenshot:

As mentioned in the previous chapter, the new window shows an empty cell for you to enter Python code.

Let's give the new work area a name, `Learning Jupyter Chapter 2`. Autosave should be on (as you can see next to the title). With an accurate name, we can find this section again easily from the notebook home page. If you select your browser's **Home** tab and refresh, you will see this new window name displayed, as shown in the following screenshot:

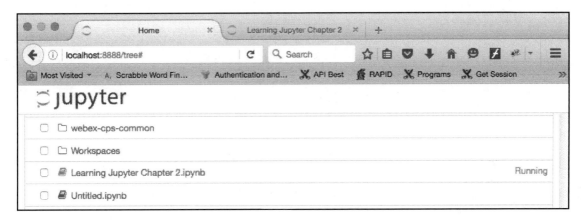

Note, it has an item icon versus a folder icon. The automatically assigned extension is IPYNB (IPython Notebook). And since the item is in a browser in a Jupyter environment, it is marked as running. There is a file by that name in your directory on disk as well, as shown in the following screenshot:

If you open the IPYNB file in a text editor, you will see the basic contents of a Jupyter node (as mentioned in the *Notebook structure* section in the previous chapter). We have one empty cell and metadata about the notebook:

```
{
  "cells": [
    {
      "cell_type": "code",
      "execution_count": null,
      "metadata": {
        "collapsed": true},
```

```
        "outputs": [],
        "source": []
      }
    ],
    "metadata": {
      "kernelspec": {
      "display_name": "Python 2",
      "language": "python",
      "name": "python2"
      },
      "language_info": {
      "codemirror_mode": {
        "name": "ipython",
        "version": 2
      },
        "file_extension": ".py",
        "mimetype": "text/x-python",
        "name": "python",
        "nbconvert_exporter": "python",
        "pygments_lexer": "ipython2",
        "version": "2.7.11"
      }
    },
    "nbformat": 4,
    "nbformat_minor": 0
  }
```

We can now enter Python coding into cells:

1. Type in some Python in the first cell.
2. Add another cell to the end (using **Insert** | **Insert Cell Below** the menu command):

   ```
   name = "Dan"
   age = 37
   ```

3. In the second cell, we enter Python code that references the variables from the first cell:

   ```
   print(name + ' is ' + str(age) + ' years old.')
   ```

4. We have this display:

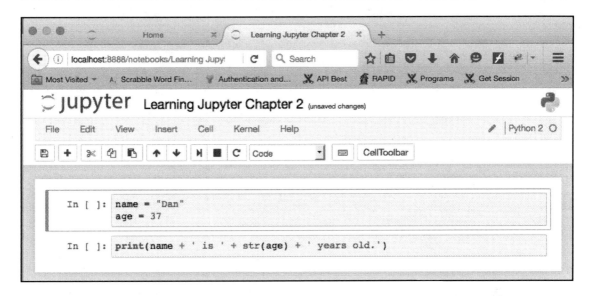

Note that Jupyter color-codes your Python (just as a decent editor would) and we have empty braces to the left of each code block.

If we execute **Cell** | **Run All Cells**, the results are displayed inline:

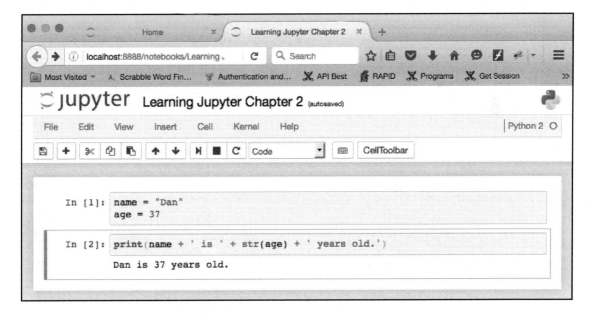

We now have the braces filled in with cell numbers, and the output of cells is appended to the bottom of each cell. It's important to note that cell 2 was able to reference variables declared in cell 1.

If we either wait for autosave to kick in or hit the save icon (the leftmost icon of a diskette) we will update the IPYNB file on disk with our results:

```
{
  "cells": [
    {
      "cell_type": "code",
      "execution_count": 1,
      "metadata": {
        "collapsed": true
      },
      "outputs": [],
      "source": [
        "name = "Dan"\n",
        "age = 37"
      ]
    },
    {
      "cell_type": "code",
      "execution_count": 2,
      "metadata": {
        "collapsed": false
      },
      "outputs": [
        {
          "name": "stdout",
          "output_type": "stream",
          "text": [
          "Dan is 37 years old.\n"
          ]
        }
      ],
      "source": [
        "print(name + ' is ' + str(age) + ' years old.')"
      ]
    }
  ],
... metadata as above
}
```

It's interesting that Jupyter keeps track of the output last generated in the saved version of the file and in saved checkpoints. You can also clear the output using the **Cell** | **All Ouput** | **Clear** command.

If you were then to re-run your cells (using **Cell** | **Run All**), the output would be regenerated (and saved via autosave). The cell numbering is incremented if you do this–Jupyter is keeping track of the latest version of each cell.

Similarly, if you were to close the browser tab, refresh the display in the **Home** tab, find the new item we created (Learning Jupyter Chapter 2.pynb), and click on it, the new tab (as created previously) will be displayed, showing the outputs that we generated when last run.

If you open the server command-line window (where the Jupyter service is running) you see a listing of the actions that we have made during our session, as shown in the following screenshot:

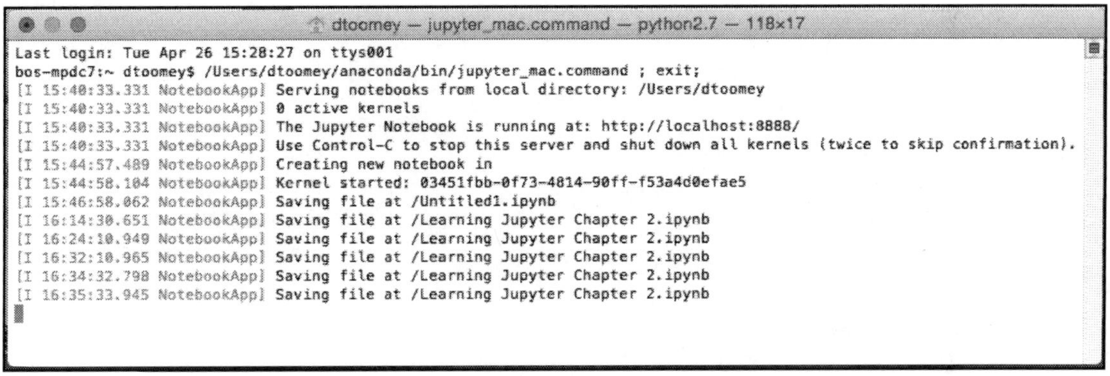

```
Last login: Tue Apr 26 15:28:27 on ttys001
bos-mpdc7:~ dtoomey$ /Users/dtoomey/anaconda/bin/jupyter_mac.command ; exit;
[I 15:40:33.331 NotebookApp] Serving notebooks from local directory: /Users/dtoomey
[I 15:40:33.331 NotebookApp] 0 active kernels
[I 15:40:33.331 NotebookApp] The Jupyter Notebook is running at: http://localhost:8888/
[I 15:40:33.331 NotebookApp] Use Control-C to stop this server and shut down all kernels (twice to skip confirmation).
[I 15:44:57.489 NotebookApp] Creating new notebook in
[I 15:44:58.104 NotebookApp] Kernel started: 03451fbb-0f73-4814-90ff-f53a4d0efae5
[I 15:46:58.062 NotebookApp] Saving file at /Untitled1.ipynb
[I 16:14:30.651 NotebookApp] Saving file at /Learning Jupyter Chapter 2.ipynb
[I 16:24:10.949 NotebookApp] Saving file at /Learning Jupyter Chapter 2.ipynb
[I 16:32:10.965 NotebookApp] Saving file at /Learning Jupyter Chapter 2.ipynb
[I 16:34:32.798 NotebookApp] Saving file at /Learning Jupyter Chapter 2.ipynb
[I 16:35:33.945 NotebookApp] Saving file at /Learning Jupyter Chapter 2.ipynb
```

The logging entries are at a high level. There may be a way to increase the logging level if there is some difficulty being encountered.

Python data access in Jupyter

Now that we have seen how Python works in Jupyter, including the underlying encoding, then how does Python accessing a large dataset work in Jupyter?

I started another view for pandas using `Python Data Access` as the name. From here, we will read in a large dataset and compute some standard statistics on the data. We are interested in seeing how we use pandas in Jupyter, how well the script performs, and what information is stored in the metadata (especially if it is a larger dataset).

Our script accesses the `iris` dataset that's built into one of the Python packages. All we are looking to do is to read in a slightly large number of items and calculate some basic operations on the dataset. We are really interested to see how much of the data is cached in the IPYNB file

The Python code is as follows:

```
# import the datasets package
from sklearn import datasets
# pull in the iris data
iris_dataset = datasets.load_iris()
# grab the first two columns of data
X = iris_dataset.data[:, :2]
# calculate some basic statistics
x_count = len(X.flat)
x_min = X[:, 0].min() - .5
x_max = X[:, 0].max() + .5
x_mean = X[:, 0].mean()
# display our results
x_count, x_min, x_max, x_mean
```

I broke these steps into a couple of cells in Jupyter, as shown in the following screenshot:

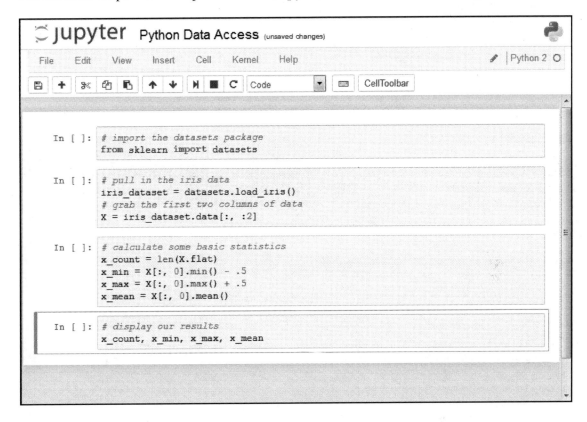

Now, run the cells (using **Cell | Run All**) and we get the following display. The only difference is the last Out line where our values are displayed:

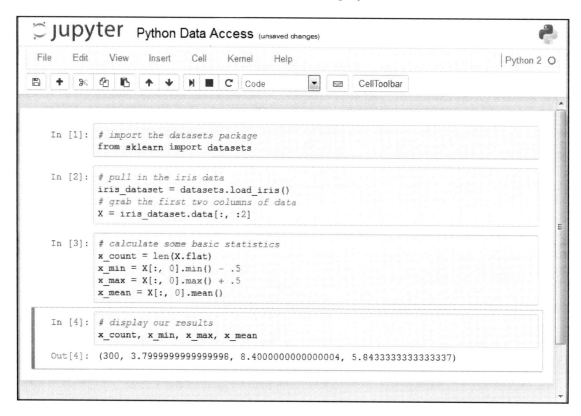

It seemed to take longer to load the library (the first time I ran the script) than to read the data and calculate the statistics.

If we look in the IPYNB file for this notebook, we see that none of the data is cached in the IPYNB file. We simply have code references to the library, our code, and the output from when we last calculated the script:

```
{
  "cell_type": "code",
  "execution_count": 4,
  "metadata": {
    "collapsed": false
  },
  "outputs": [
    {
      "data": {
```

```
        "text/plain": [
          "(300, 3.7999999999999998, 8.400000000000004,
5.8433333333333337)"
          ]
        },
      "execution_count": 4,
      "metadata": {},
      "output_type": "execute_result"
      }
    ],
    "source": [
      "# calculate some basic statistics\n",
      "x_count = len(X.flat)\n",
      "x_min = X[:, 0].min() - .5\n",
      "x_max = X[:, 0].max() + .5\n",
      "x_mean = X[:, 0].mean()\n",
      "\n",
      "# display our results\n",
      "x_count, x_min, x_max, x_mean"
    ]
  }
```

Python pandas in Jupyter

One of the most widely used features of Python is pandas. It is a third-party library of data analysis packages that can be used freely. In this example, we will develop a Python script that uses pandas to see if there is any effect to using it in Jupyter.

I am using the Titanic dataset from http://www.kaggle.com/c/titanic-gettingStarted /download/train.csv. I am sure the same data is available from a variety of sources.

Here is the Python script that we want to run in Jupyter:

```python
from pandas import *
training_set = read_csv('train.csv')
training_set.head()
male = training_set[training_set.sex == 'male']
female = training_set[training_set.sex =='female']
womens_survival_rate = float(sum(female.survived))/len(female)
mens_survival_rate = float(sum(male.survived))/len(male)
```

The result is we calculate the survival rates of the Titanic's passengers based on their sex.

We create a new notebook, enter the script into appropriate cells, include adding displays of calculated data at each point, and produce our results.

Here is our notebook laid out; we added displays of calculated data in each cell, as shown in the following screenshot:

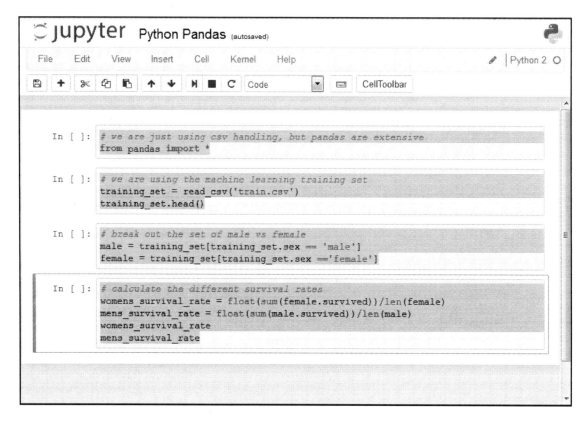

When I ran this script, I had two problems.

On Windows, it is common to use a backslash (\) to separate parts of a filename. However, this coding uses the backslash as a special character. So, I had to change over to use forward slash (/) in my CSV file path. I originally had a full path to the CSV in the preceding code example. The dataset column names are taken directly from the file and are case sensitive. In this case, I was originally using the sex field in my script, but in the CSV file, the column is named Sex. Similarly, I had to change survived to Survived.

The final script and results look like the following screenshot when we run it:

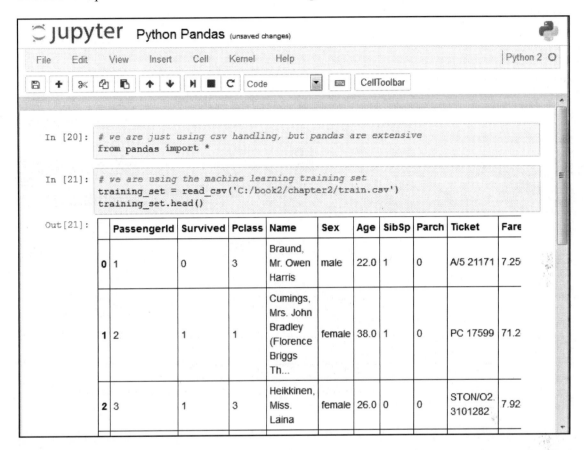

I have used the `head()` function to display the first few lines of the dataset. It is interesting to see the amount of detail that is available for all of the passengers.

If you scroll down, you see the results, as shown in the following screenshot:

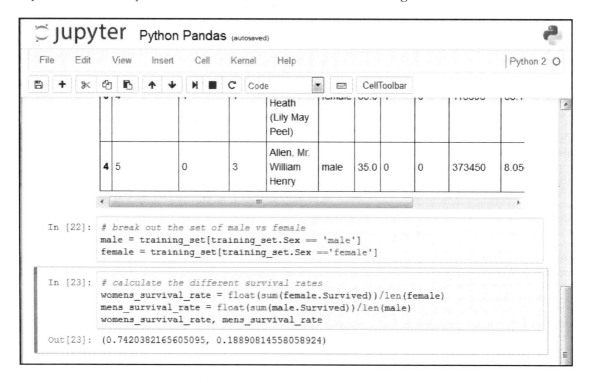

We see 74% of the survivors were women versus just 19% men. I would like to think chivalry is not dead.

It's curious the results do not add up to 100%. However, like every other dataset I have seen, there is missing and/or inaccurate data present.

Python graphics in Jupyter

How does Python graphics work in Jupyter?

I started another view for this named `Python Graphics` so as to distinguish the work from the previous work.

If we were to build a sample dataset of baby names and the number of births in a year of that name, we could then plot the data.

The Python coding is simple:

```
import pandas
import matplotlib
%matplotlib inline
baby_name = ['Alice','Charles','Diane','Edward']
number_births = [96, 155, 66, 272]
dataset = list(zip(baby_name,number_births))
df = pandas.DataFrame(data = dataset, columns=['Name', 'Number'])
df['Number'].plot()
```

The steps of the script are as follows:

1. Import the graphics library (and data library) that we need.
2. Define our data.
3. Convert the data into a format that allows easy graphical display.
4. Plot the data.

We would expect a graph of the number of births by baby name.

If we take the preceding script and place it into cells of our Jupyter Notebook, we get something that looks like the following screenshot:

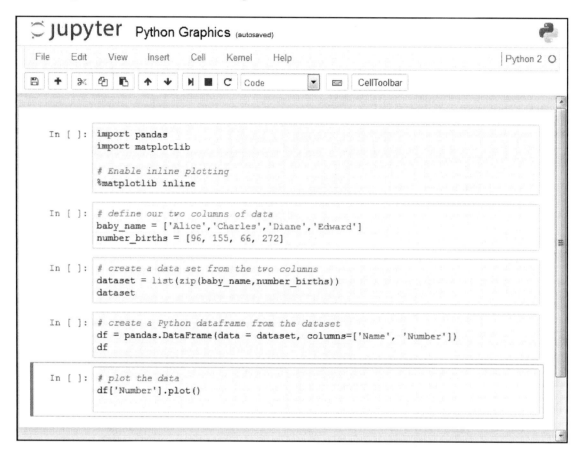

I have broken the script into different cells for easier readability. Having different cells also allows you to develop the script easily step by step, and you can display the values computed so far to validate your results. I have done this in most of the cells by displaying the `dataset` and `DataFrame` at the bottom of those cells.

When we run this script (**Cell | Run All**), we see the results at each step displayed as the script progresses:

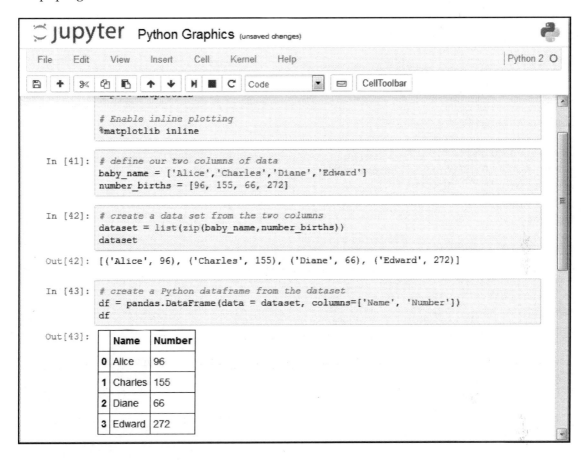

And finally, we see our plot of the `births`, as shown in the following screenshot:

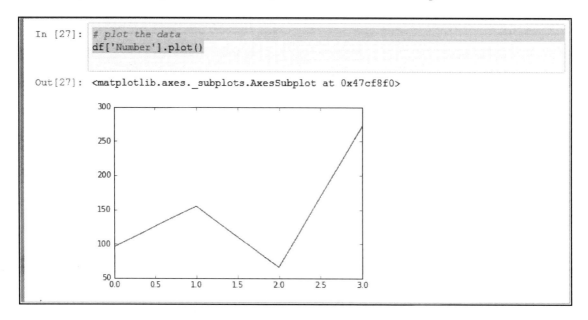

I was curious what metadata was stored for this script. Looking into the IPYNB file, you can see the expected value for the formula cells.

The tabular data display of the `DataFrame` is stored as HTML—convenient:

```
{
  "cell_type": "code",
  "execution_count": 43,
  "metadata": {
    "collapsed": false
  },
  "outputs": [
    {
      "data": {
        "text/html": [
          "<div>\n",
            "<table border=\"1\" class=\"dataframe\">\n",
              "<thead>\n",
                "<tr style=\"text-align: right;\">\n",
                "<th></th>\n",
                "<th>Name</th>\n",
                "<th>Number</th>\n",
                "</tr>\n",
              "</thead>\n",
```

```
            "<tbody>\n",
              "<tr>\n",
              "<th>0</th>\n",
              "<td>Alice</td>\n",
              "<td>96</td>\n",
              "</tr>\n",
              "<tr>\n",
              "<th>1</th>\n",
              "<td>Charles</td>\n",
              "<td>155</td>\n",
              "</tr>\n",
              "<tr>\n",
              "<th>2</th>\n",
              "<td>Diane</td>\n",
              "<td>66</td>\n",
              "</tr>\n",
              "<tr>\n",
              "<th>3</th>\n",
              "<td>Edward</td>\n",
              "<td>272</td>\n",
              "</tr>\n",
            "</tbody>\n",
          "</table>\n",
        "</div>"
      ],
        "text/plain": [
        "       Name  Number\n",
        "0     Alice      96\n",
        "1   Charles     155\n",
        "2     Diane      66\n",
        "3    Edward     272"
        ]
    },
    "execution_count": 43,
    "metadata": {},
    "output_type": "execute_result"
  }
 ],
(... continued as above)
}
```

The graphic output cell is stored like this:

```
{
  "cell_type": "code",
  "execution_count": 27,
  "metadata": {
    "collapsed": false
```

```
    },
    "outputs": [
      {
        "data": {
          "text/plain": [
            "<matplotlib.axes._subplots.AxesSubplot at 0x47cf8f0>"
          ]
        },
        "execution_count": 27,
        "metadata": {},
        "output_type": "execute_result"
      },
      {
        "data": {
          "image/png":
          "<a few hundred lines of hexcodes>
          .../wc/B0RRYEH0EQAAAABJRU5ErkJggg==\n",
          "text/plain": [
          "<matplotlib.figure.Figure at 0x47d8e30>"
          ]
        },
        "metadata": {},
        "output_type": "display_data"
      }
    ],
    "source": [
      "# plot the data\n",
      "df['Number'].plot()\n"
    ]
  }
], (... similar coding as above for the file trailer)
```

The `"image/png"` tag contains a large hex digit string representation of the graphical image displayed on screen (I abbreviated the display in the coding shown). So, the actual generated image is stored in the metadata for the page.

So, rather than a cache, Jupyter is remembering the output from when each cell was last executed.

Python random numbers in Jupyter

For many analyses, we are interested in calculating repeatable results. However, a lot of analysis relies on random numbers being used. In Python, you can set the seed for the random number generator to achieve repeatable results with the `random_seed()` function.

In this example, we simulate rolling a pair of dice and looking at the outcome.

The script we are using is this:

```
import pylab
import random
random.seed(113)
samples = 1000
dice = []
for i in range(samples):
    total = random.randint(1,6) + random.randint(1,6)
    dice.append(total)
pylab.hist(dice, bins= pylab.arange(1.5,12.6,1.0))
pylab.show()
```

Once we have the script in Jupyter and execute it, we have this result:

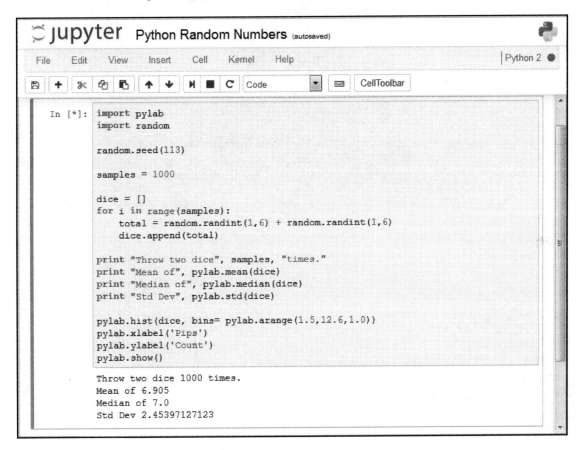

I had added some more statistics. I'm not sure I would have counted on such a high standard deviation. If we increased the number of samples, this would increase.

The resulting graph was opened in a new window, much as it would be if you ran this script in another Python development environment:

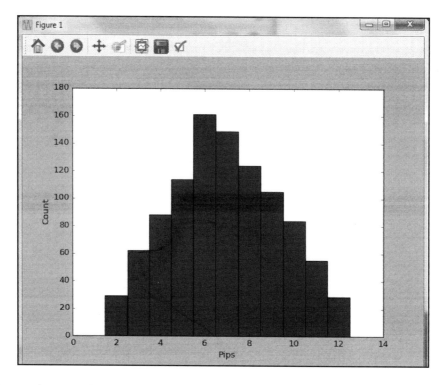

The toolbar at the top of the graphic is extensive, allowing you to manipulate the graphic in many ways.

Summary

In this chapter, we walked through a simple notebook and the underlying structure. Then, we saw an example of using pandas. We looked at a graphics example. Finally, we looked at an example using random numbers in a Python script.

In the next chapter, we will learn all about R scripting in a Jupyter Notebook.

3
Jupyter R Scripting

Jupyter's native language is Python. Once Jupyter (essentially, IPython before being renamed) became popular for data analysis, a number of people were interested in using the suite of R programming analysis tools that are available in a Jupyter Notebook.

In this chapter, we will cover the following topics:

- Adding R scripting to your installation
- Basic R scripting
- R dataset access (from a library)
- R graphics
- R cluster analysis
- R forecasting

Adding R scripting to your installation

Two big installation platforms are Mac and Windows. There are separate, but similar, steps required to make R scripting available in your Jupyter installation.

Adding R scripts to Jupyter on a Mac

If you are operating a Mac, you can add R scripting using the command-line:

```
conda install -c r r-essentials
```

This will start off with a large installation of the R environment, which contains a number of common packages:

```
bos-mpdc7:~ dtoomey$ conda install -c r r-essentials
Fetching package metadata: ......
Solving package specifications: ........
Package plan for installation in environment /Users/dtoomey/miniconda3:
The following packages will be downloaded:
        package                    |                build
        ---------------------------|------------------
        jbig-2.1                   |                    0          31 KB
        jpeg-8d                    |                    2         210 KB
        libgcc-4.8.5               |                    1         785 KB
    ... <<many packages>>
        r-caret-6.0_62             |          r3.2.2_0a         4.3 MB
        r-essentials-1.1           |          r3.2.2_1a         726 B
        ------------------------------------------------------------
                                                Total:        101.0 MB
The following NEW packages will be INSTALLED:
        jbig:         2.1-0
        jpeg:         8d-2
    ... <<many packages>>
        r-xts:        0.9_7-r3.2.2_0a
        r-yaml:       2.1.13-r3.2.2_1a
        r-zoo:        1.7_12-r3.2.2_1a
        zeromq:       4.1.3-0
Proceed ([y]/n)? y
Fetching packages ...
    jbig-2.1-0.tar 100% |############################| Time: 0:00:00
1.59 MB/s
    jpeg-8d-2.tar. 100% |############################| Time: 0:00:00
2.69 MB/s
    ... <<many packages>>
    r-caret-6.0_62 100% |############################| Time: 0:00:00
11.16 MB/s
    r-essentials-1 100% |############################| Time: 0:00:00
537.43 kB/s
    Extracting packages ...
    [        COMPLETE
]|############################################| 100%
    Linking packages ...
    [        COMPLETE
]|############################################| 100%
```

From there, you invoke your notebook as you normally would:

```
ipython notebook
```

Adding R scripts to Jupyter on Windows

If you are operating a Windows machine, you are in for quite a few steps to get R in Jupyter. This environment was really developed for Linux.

On my machine, Anaconda was installed in my user directory. This is probably because I selected to install it just for myself. If you open a command-line window in the Anaconda/scripts directory, you should first make sure your notebook software is up to date using the following command:

```
conda update notebook
```

This produces the following output (for me — your results may be different so as to update different aspects as needed):

```
C:\Users\Dan\Anaconda2\Scripts>conda update notebook
Using Anaconda Cloud api site https://api.anaconda.org
Fetching package metadata: ....
Solving package specifications: ........
Package plan for installation in environment C:\Users\Dan\Anaconda2:
The following packages will be downloaded:
    package                    |              build
    ---------------------------|-----------------
    notebook-4.2.0             |              py27_0         5.2 MB
The following packages will be updated:
    notebook: 4.1.0-py27_2 --> 4.2.0-py27_0
Proceed ([y]/n)? y
Fetching packages ...
notebook-4.2.0 100% |#############################| Time: 0:00:04
1.12 MB/s
    Extracting packages ...
    [      COMPLETE      ] |#######################################| 100%
Unlinking packages ...
    [      COMPLETE      ] |#######################################| 100%
Linking packages ...
    [      COMPLETE      ] |#######################################| 100%
```

Then we take the plunge and add R scripting:

```
conda install -c r notebook r-irkernel
```

This produces a detailed view of the packages that are updated. In my case, it installed a full set of R packages and runtimes even though I had used R elsewhere on the machine earlier:

```
C:\Users\Dan\Anaconda2\Scripts>conda install -c r notebook r-irkernel
Using Anaconda Cloud api site https://api.anaconda.org
Fetching package metadata: ......
Solving package specifications: ........
Package plan for installation in environment C:\Users\Dan\Anaconda2:
The following packages will be downloaded:
        package                    |               build
        ---------------------------|-----------------
        msys2-conda-epoch-20160418 |                0          420 B
        m2w64-expat-2.1.1          |                1          164 KB
        m2w64-gmp-6.1.0            |                1          638 KB
        m2w64-gsl-2.1             |                1          2.3 MB
...  <<many packages>>
        r-evaluate-0.8.3          |          r3.2.4_0           44 KB
        r-irkernel-0.6            |          r3.2.4_0           78 KB
        -------------------------------------------------------------
                                              Total:         100.5 MB
The following NEW packages will be INSTALLED:
        m2w64-bwidget:       1.9.10-1
        m2w64-bzip2:         1.0.6-5
        m2w64-expat:         2.1.1-1
        r-stringi:           1.0_1-r3.2.4_0
        r-stringr:           1.0.0-r3.2.4_0
        r-survival:          2.38_3-r3.2.4_0
        r-uuid:              0.1_2-r3.2.4_0
...  <<many packages>>
Proceed ([y]/n)? y
Fetching packages ...
msys2-conda-ep 100% |####################| Time: 0:00:00   26.25 kB/s
m2w64-expat-2. 100% |####################| Time: 0:00:00    1.19 MB/s
m2w64-gmp-6.1. 100% |####################| Time: 0:00:00    1.90 MB/s
m2w64-gsl-2.1- 100% |####################| Time: 0:00:00    3.27 MB/s
m2w64-libiconv 100% |####################| Time: 0:00:00    2.82 MB/s
...  <<many packages>>
r-evaluate-0.8 100% |####################| Time: 0:00:00 964.72 kB/s
r-irkernel-0.6 100% |####################| Time: 0:00:00 508.94 kB/s
Extracting packages ...
[         COMPLETE      ]|######################################| 100%
Linking packages ...
[         COMPLETE      ]|######################################| 100%
```

Adding R packages to Jupyter

The standard installation for R under Jupyter has many packages that are commonly used in R programming. However, if you do need to add another package, it is a small number of steps:

1. Close down your notebook (including the server).
2. In the command-line window, type the following:

```
R
install.packages("name of the R package you want to add")
quit()
# answer Yes to save
```

3. Restart your notebook, and the package should be available for use in your R script. To use an installed package, type `library`(name of the R package you want to add).

Note, you may still have problems in R if the core version of R that you have installed is out of date and you need to upgrade to use a particular library.

R limitations in Jupyter

In this chapter, we used a variety of packages, both pre-installed and installed especially for the example. I have exercised a variety of materials available in R under Jupyter and have not found any limitations; you can do most of the steps in Jupyter that you would have done under the standard R implementations. The only limitation appears to be when you are using **Shiny** or if you are attempting to use extensive markdown:

- For Shiny, I think you are mixing purposes–Jupyter provides a web experience and so does Shiny–so I'm not sure how to even decide if this should work. This issue is being addressed by the Jupyter development group.
- Using extensive markdown also does not appear to be a good idea. The intent of markdown was to allow notebook developers to augment the standard output (of R) in a more illustrative manner. I think if you are adding extensive markdown to your notebook you really need to develop a website, maybe using Shiny–then you would have all HTML markdown available.

After adding R scripts to Jupyter

Once the notebook is up and running (you should be able to use the command-line `jupyter notebook`), if you open the **New** menu in the top-right, you will see a choice has been added for R scripting:

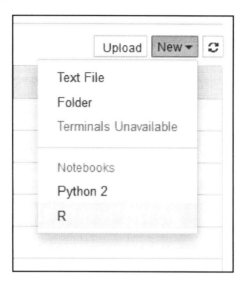

Basic R in Jupyter

Start a new **R** notebook and call it `R Basics`. We can enter a small script just so we can see how the steps progress for an R script. Enter the following into separate cells of your notebook:

```
myString <- "Hello, World!"
print (myString)
```

You will end up with a starting screen that looks like this:

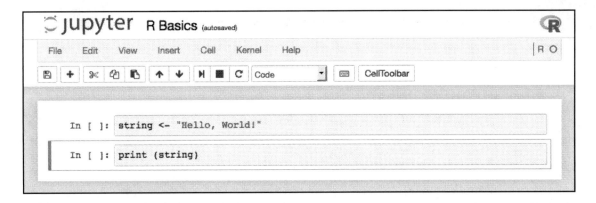

We should note the aspects of the R notebook view:

- We have the R logo in the upper-right corner. You will see this logo running in other R installations.
- There is also the peculiar **R O** just below the R icon. The unfilled circle indicates that the kernel is at rest, and the filled circle indicates the kernel is working.
- The rest of the menu items are the same as we have seen before.

This is a very simple script–set a variable in one cell then print out its value in another cell. Once executed (**Cell** | **Run All**), you will see your results:

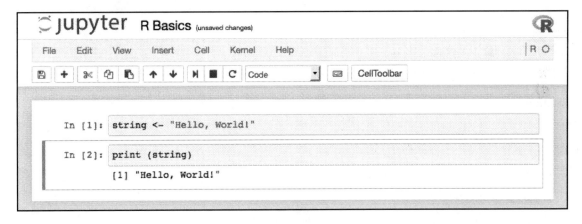

So, just as if you ran the script in an R interpreter, you get your output (with the numerical prefix). Jupyter has counted the statements so we have incremental numbering of the cells. Jupyter has not done anything special to print out variables for debugging, you would have to do that separately.

If we look at the R server-logging statements (a command-line window was created when we started Jupyter), we see the actions that took place:

```
$ jupyter notebook
[I 11:00:06.965 NotebookApp] Serving notebooks from local directory:
/Users/dtoomey/miniconda3/bin
[I 11:00:06.965 NotebookApp] 0 active kernels
[I 11:00:06.965 NotebookApp] The Jupyter Notebook is running at:
http://localhost:8888/
[I 11:00:06.965 NotebookApp] Use Control-C to stop this server and shut
down all kernels (twice to skip confirmation).
[I 11:00:17.447 NotebookApp] Creating new notebook in
[I 11:00:18.199 NotebookApp] Kernel started:
518308da-460a-4eb9-9959-1411e31dec69
[1] "Got unhandled msg_type:" "comm_open"
[I 11:02:18.160 NotebookApp] Saving file at /Untitled.ipynb
[I 11:08:27.340 NotebookApp] Saving file at /R Basics.ipynb
[1] "Got unhandled msg_type:" "comm_open"
[I 11:14:45.204 NotebookApp] Saving file at /R Basics.ipynb
```

We started the server, created a new notebook, and saved it as R Basics. If we open the IPYNB file on disk (using a text editor), we can see the following:

```
{
  "cells": [
    ...<similar to previously displayed>
  ],
  "metadata": {
    "kernelspec": {
      "display_name": "R",
      "language": "R",
      "name": "ir"
    },
    "language_info": {
      "codemirror_mode": "r",
      "file_extension": ".r",
      "mimetype": "text/x-r-source",
      "name": "R",
      "pygments_lexer": "r",
      "version": "3.2.2"
    }
  },
  ...<omitted>
}
```

This is a little different than what we saw in the prior chapter on Python notebook coding. Particularly, the metadata clearly tells the script cells to be R script. Note, the actual cells are not specific to a language–they are just scripts that will be executed as per the metadata directives.

R dataset access

For this example, we will use the **Iris** dataset. Iris is built into R installations and is available directly. Let's just pull in the data, gather some simple statistics, and plot the data. This will show R accessing a dataset in Jupyter, using an R built-in package, as well as some available statistics (since we have R), and the interaction with R graphics.

The script we will use is as follows:

```
dataset(iris)
summary(iris)
plot(iris)
```

If we enter this small script into a new R notebook, we get an initial display that looks like the following:

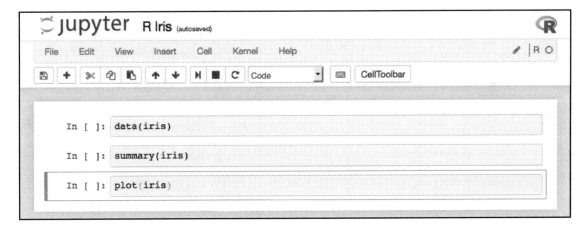

I would expect the standard R statistical summary as output, and I know the Iris plot is pretty interesting. We can see exactly what happened in the following screenshot:

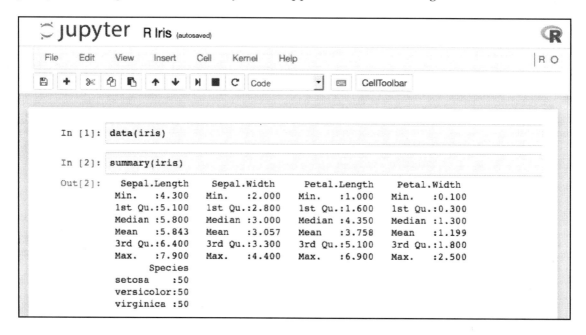

The plot continues in the following screenshot as it wouldn't fit into a single screenshot:

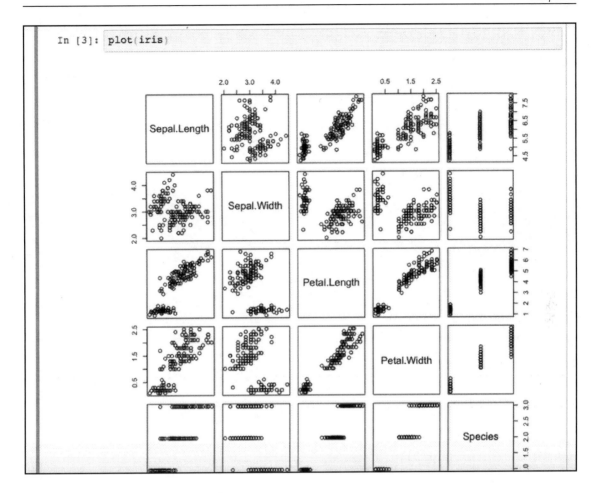

```
In [3]: plot(iris)
```

R visualizations in Jupyter

A common use of R is to use several visualizations, which are available depending on the underlying data. In this section, we will go over some of them to see how R interacts with Jupyter.

R 3D graphics in Jupyter

One of the packages available for 3D graphics is `persp`. The `persp` package draws perspective plots over a 2D space.

We can enter a basic `persp` command in a new notebook and have something like this:

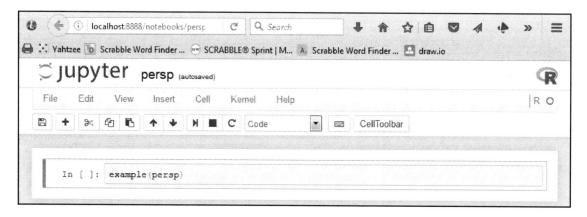

Once we run the step (**Cell | Run All**), we can see the display in the following screenshot. The first part is the script involved to generate the graphic (this is part of the example code):

In [1]: example(persp)

```
persp> require(grDevices) # for trans3d

persp> ## More examples in  demo(persp) !!
persp> ##                   -----------
persp>
persp> # (1) The Obligatory Mathematical surface.
persp> #     Rotated sinc function.
persp>
persp> x <- seq(-10, 10, length= 30)

persp> y <- x

persp> f <- function(x, y) { r <- sqrt(x^2+y^2); 10 * sin(r)/r }

persp> z <- outer(x, y, f)

persp> z[is.na(z)] <- 1

persp> op <- par(bg = "white")

persp> persp(x, y, z, theta = 30, phi = 30, expand = 0.5, col = "lightblue"
)

persp> persp(x, y, z, theta = 30, phi = 30, expand = 0.5, col = "lightblue"
```

Then we see the following graphic display:

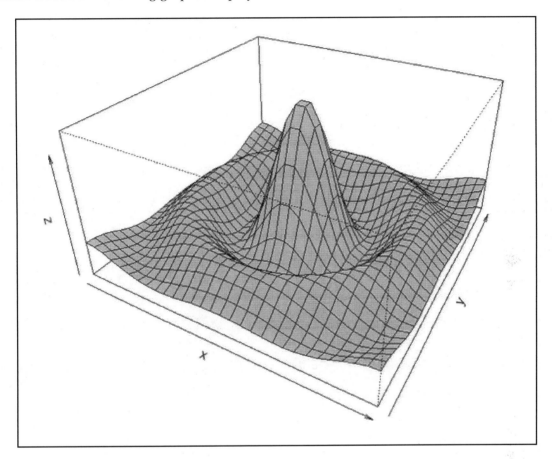

R 3D scatterplot in Jupyter

The R lattice package has a cloud function that will produce 3D scatterplots.

The script we will use is as follows:

```
# make sure lattice package is installed
install.package("lattice")
# in a standalone R script you would have a command to download the
lattice library - this is not needed in Jupyter
library("lattice")
# use the automobile data from ics.edu
mydata <-
```

```
read.table("http://archive.ics.uci.edu/ml/machine-learning-databases/auto-m
pg/auto-mpg.data")
    # define more meaningful column names for the display
    colnames(mydata) <- c("mpg", "cylinders", "displacement", "horsepower",
"weight", "acceleration", "model.year", "origin", "car.name")
    # 3-D plot with number of cylinders on x axis, weight of the vehicle on
the y axis and miles per gallon on the z axis.
    cloud(mpg~cylinders*weight, data=mydata)
```

Prior to running, we have something like this:

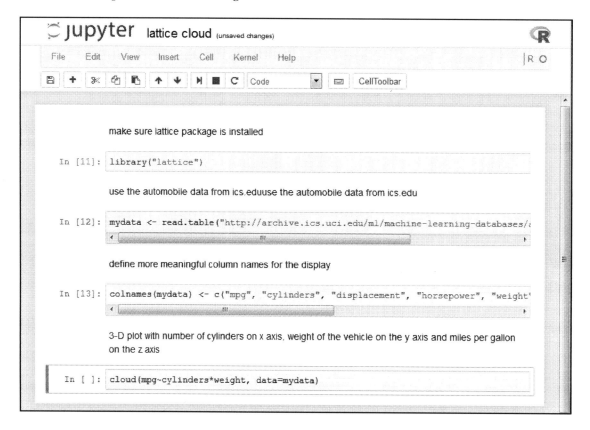

Notice, we are using markup type cells for comments about the script steps. They are also denoted without a script line number in the left-hand column.

If you are copying R script into a Jupyter window, you may run across an issue where the print copy you are using has non-standard double quote characters (quotes on the left lean to the left, quotes on the right lean to the right). Once copied into Jupyter, you need to change this to normal double quotes (they don't lean but are vertical).

After running this, we see the following display:

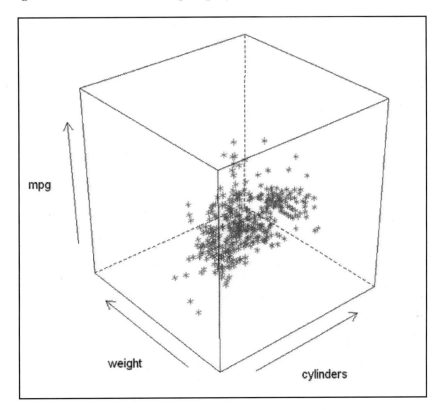

R cluster analysis

In this example, we use R's cluster analysis functions to determine the clustering in the wheat dataset from `http://www.ics.uci.edu/`.

The R script we want to use in Jupyter is the following:

```
# load the wheat data set from uci.edu
wheat <-
read.csv("http://archive.ics.uci.edu/ml/machine-learning-databases/00236/se
eds_dataset.txt", sep="\t")
# define useful column names
colnames(wheat) <-c("area", "perimeter", "compactness", "length",
"width", "asymmetry", "groove", "undefined")
# exclude incomplete cases from the data
wheat <- wheat[complete.cases(wheat),]
# calculate the clusters
fit <- kmeans(wheat, 5)
fit
```

Once entered into a notebook, we have something like this:

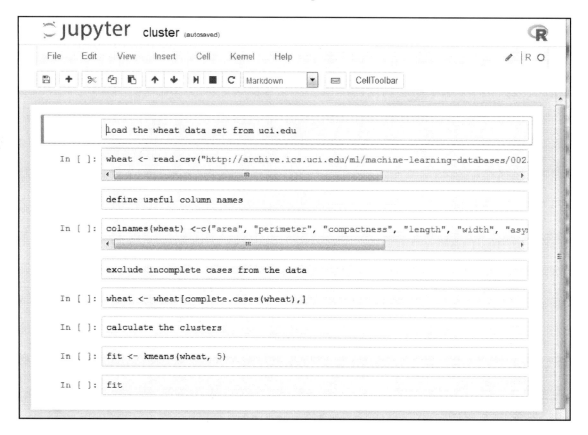

The resulting generated cluster information is K-means clustering with five clusters of sizes 29, 57, 65, 15, and 32. (Note that, since I had not set the seed value for random number to use, your results may vary.)

Cluster means are:

```
       area perimeter compactness   length    width asymmetry
1 16.45345  15.35310   0.8768000 5.882655 3.462517  3.913207
2 14.06456  14.17175   0.8788158 5.463825 3.211526  2.496354
3 11.91292  13.26692   0.8496292 5.237477 2.857908  4.844477
4 19.58333  16.64600   0.8877267 6.315867 3.835067  5.081533
5 18.95781  16.39563   0.8862125 6.250469 3.742781  2.719813
```

Clustering vectors are:

```
      1   2   3   4   5   6   9  10  11  12  13  14  15  16  17  18  19  20
21 22
      2   2   2   2   2   2   1   1   1   2   2   2   2   2   2   2   2   2
 2  2
  . . .
```

Within cluster sum of squares by cluster are:

```
[1]   54.16095 146.71080 147.29278   25.81297   30.06596
 (between_SS / total_SS =   85.0 %)
```

The available components are:

```
[1] "cluster"      "centers"     "totss"        "withinss"
"tot.withinss"
[6] "betweenss"    "size"        "iter"         "ifault"
```

So, we generated information about five clusters (the parameter passed in the `fit` statement).

R forecasting

For this example, we will forecast the Fraser River levels given the data from https://data market.com/data/set/22nm/fraser-river-at-hope-1913-1990#!ds=22nm&display=line . I was not able to find a suitable source so I extracted the data by hand from the site into a local file.

We will be using the R forecast package. You have to add this package to your setup (as described at the start of this chapter).

The R script we will be using is as follows:

```
library(forecast)
fraser <- scan("fraser.txt")
plot(fraser)
fraser.ts <- ts(fraser, frequency=12, start=c(1913,3))
fraser.stl = stl(fraser.ts, s.window="periodic")
monthplot(fraser.stl)
seasonplot(fraser.ts)
```

The output of interest in this example are the three plots: simple plot, monthly, and computed seasonal.

The simple plot (using the R `plot` command) is like the following screenshot. There is no apparent organization or structure:

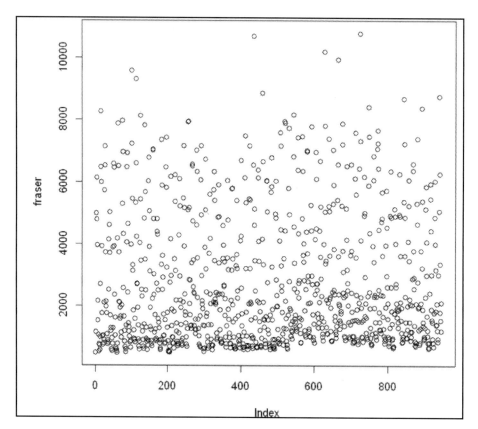

The monthly plot (using the `monthplot` command) is like the following screenshot. River flows appear to be very consistent within a month:

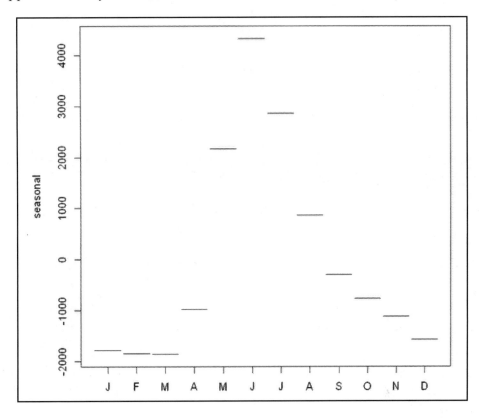

Finally, the seasonal plot shows quite dramatically what we have been trying to forecast, that is, definite seasonality to the river flows:

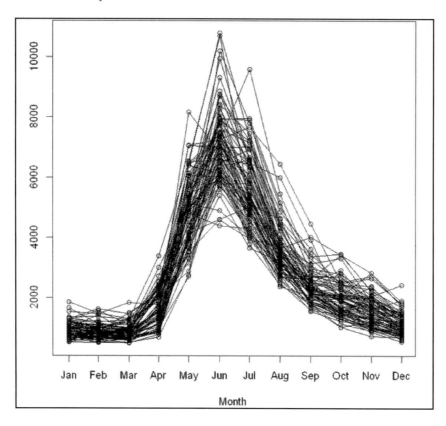

Summary

In this chapter, we added the ability to use R scripts in your Jupyter Notebook. We added an R library not included in the standard R installation and we made a `Hello World` script in R. We then saw R data access built-in libraries and some of the simpler graphics and statistics that are automatically generated. We used an R script to generate 3D graphics in a couple of different ways. We then performed a standard cluster analysis (which I think is one of the basic uses of R) and used one of the available forecasting tools.

In the next chapter, we will learn all about Julia scripting in a Jupyter Notebook.

4
Jupyter Julia Scripting

Julia is a language specifically designed to be used for high performance, numerical computing. Most importantly, it differs from the previous scripting languages covered in this book (R and, to a certain extent, Python) in that Julia is a full language, not limited to data handling.

In this chapter, we will cover the following topics:

- Adding Julia scripting to your installation
- Basic Julia in Jupyter
- Julia limitations in Jupyter
- Standard Julia capabilities
- Julia visualizations in Jupyter
- Julia Vega plotting
- Julia parallel processing
- Julia control flow
- Julia regular expressions
- Julia unit testing

Adding Julia scripting to your installation

We will install on Mac and Windows. There are separate steps for making Julia scripting available in your Jupyter installation.

Adding Julia scripts to Jupyter on a Mac

If you are running on a Mac, you are in luck. The Mac installation of Jupyter includes Julia 0.4.5, as can be seen in the **New** menu:

Adding Julia scripts to Jupyter on Windows

If you are running on a Windows machine, there are a few steps to get Julia on Jupyter. Remember, this environment was really developed for Linux.

First, we need to install Julia on your Windows machine. Navigate to the Julia download page (http://julialang.org/downloads/), download the correct version, which is Julia 0.4.5 for Windows (in my case, I used the Windows self-extracting EXE file for 32-bit machines), and run the installation with standard defaults.

You must run the Julia installation as Administrator on your machine. After downloading the file, open the Downloads folder, right-click on the Julia executable, and select **Run as administrator**.

Once the install is complete, you should verify that everything worked. Select Julia from the programs list and run the Julia program. You should see the Julia command-line, as shown in the following screenshot:

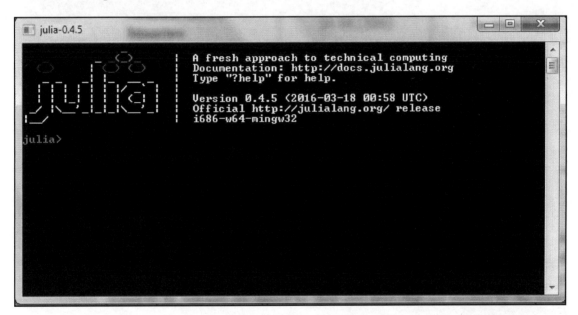

In the Julia window, run the following command to add Julia to Jupyter:

```
Pkg.add("IJulia")
```

This will result in **IJulia** (Interactive Julia) being downloaded and installed on your machine. There are many sub-packages that will get automatically installed as well. Your display will look something like the following screenshot:

Julia uses font color as feedback. I entered the text `Pkg.add` in white at the top of the screen, successful execution steps are in blue, and possible problems are shown in red. You must wait for the installation to complete. The last line should have read as follows:

```
INFO: Package database updated
```

At this point, you can close the Julia window (using the `quit()` command).

One last step is to open your notebook (using the `jupyter notebook` command), and if you open the **New** menu (in the upper-right corner of the screen), you should see a Julia type available as shown in the following screenshot:

Adding Julia packages to Jupyter

The standard installation for Julia in Jupyter has many packages that are commonly used in Julia programming. However, if you do need to add another package, it is a small number of steps:

1. Close down your notebook (including the server).
2. Run the Julia command-line program and type the following:

```
Pkg.add("DataFrames")
Pkg.add("RDatasets")
Pkg.add("Gadfly")
quit();
```

3. Restart your notebook and the package should be available in your Julia script. To use an installed package, type `library`(name of the R package you want to add).

I would recommend adding the three preceding packages right away as they are needed for many scripts.

 The first time you use a package in Julia you will see a line highlighted in light red that shows Julia is precompiling, such as this:

```
INFO: Precompiling module Dataframes...
```

You can use the `Pkg.add(...)` function directly in your script, but that doesn't seem correct. Every time you run your script, the system will attempt to validate whether you have the specified package or not, install it into your environment if needed, and even tell you if you are out of date. None of these steps belong as part of your script.

Basic Julia in Jupyter

In this example we will use the Iris dataset for some standard analysis. So, start a new Julia notebook and call it `Julia Iris`. We can enter a small script to see how the steps progress for a Julia script.

This script uses another package for plotting, `Gadfly`. You would have to go through similar steps as before to install the package before operating the script.

Enter the following script into separate cells of your notebook:

```
using RDatasets, DataFrames, Gadfly
set_default_plot_size(5inch, 5inch/golden);
plot(dataset("datasets","iris"), x="SepalWidth",
    y="SepalLength", color="Species")
```

`RDataSets` is a library containing several of the commonly used R datasets, such as Iris. This is a simple script–we define our libraries that we are going to use, set the size of the plot area, and plot out the Iris data points (color coded to species).

So, you would end up with a starting screen that looks like the following screenshot:

We should take note of a few aspects of the Julia notebook view:

- We have the Julia logo (the three colored circles) in the upper-right corner. You will have seen this logo running in other Julia installations (as we saw earlier when we ran the Julia command line).
- The circle to the right of the Julia logo is a busy indicator. When your script starts, the title of the table says **Busy** as Julia is starting. When your script is running, the circle is filled in black. When it is not running, it is empty.
- The rest of the menu items are the same as before.

 On my Windows machine, it took quite a while for the Julia notebook to start the first time. The **Kernel starting, please wait...** message was displayed for several minutes.

If you run the script (using the **Cell | Run All** menu command), your output should look like the following screenshot:

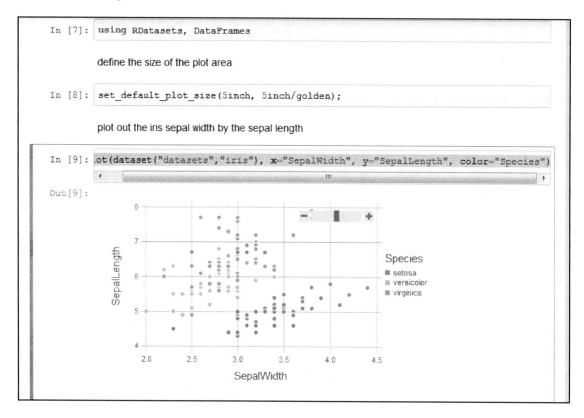

I noticed that if you hover the mouse over a graphic, you get grid lines displayed and a slide bar to adjust the zoom level (as shown in the upper-right part of the preceding screenshot).

So, just as if you ran the script in the Julia interpreter, you get your output (with the numerical prefix). Jupyter has counted the statements so we have incremental numbering of the cells. Jupyter has not done anything special to print out variables or the like.

We started the server, created a new notebook, and saved it as `Julia Iris`. If we open the IPYNB file on disk (using a text editor), we can see the following:

```
{
  "cells": [
    ...<similar to previously displayed>
  ],
  "metadata": {
    "kernelspec": {
      "display_name": "Julia 0.4.5",
      "language": "julia",
      "name": "julia-0.4"
    },
    "language_info": {
      "file_extension": ".jl",
      "mimetype": "application/julia",
      "name": "julia",
      "version": "0.4.5"
    }
  ...<omitted>
  }
```

This is a little different than what we saw in the previous chapters with other notebook language coding. Particularly, the metadata clearly targets the script cells to be Julia script.

Julia limitations in Jupyter

I have written Julia scripts and accessed different Julia libraries without issue in Jupyter. I have not noticed any limitations on its use or any performance degradation. I imagine some aspects of Julia that are very screen dependent (such as using the Julia Webstack to build a website) may be hampered by conflicting uses of the same concept.

I have repeatedly seen updates being run when I am attempting to run a Julia script, as in the following screenshot. I am not sure why they decided to always update the underlying tool rather than use what is in play and have the user specify whether to update libraries:

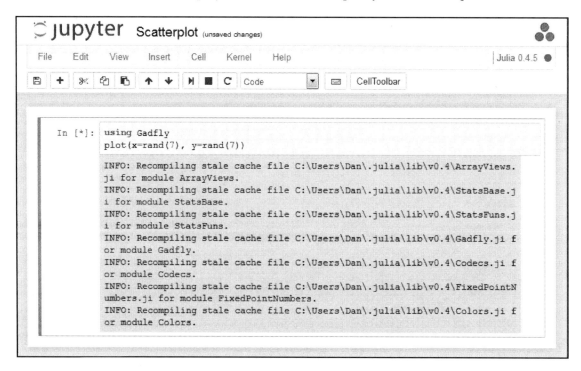

I have also noticed that once a Julia notebook is opened, even though I have closed the page, it will still display **Running** on the home page. I don't recall seeing this behavior with the other script languages available.

Another issue has been trying to use a secured package in my script, for example, `plotly`. It appears to be a clean process to get credentials, but using the prescribed methods for passing your credentials to `plotly` does not work under Windows. I am hesitant to provide examples that do not work in both environments.

Further interactions with Windows are also limited, for example, attempting to access environment variables by calls to standard C libraries that are normally not present on a Windows installation.

I have another issue with Julia itself–regardless of whether it's running in Jupyter or not. When using a package, it will complain about features that are used in the package that have been deprecated or improved. As a user of the package, I have no control over this behavior, so it does not help me in my work.

Standard Julia capabilities

Similar to functions in other languages, Julia can perform most of the rudimentary statistics on your data using the describe function, as in the example script that follows:

```
using RDatasets
describe(dataset("datasets", "iris"))
```

This script accesses the Iris dataset and displays summary statistics on the dataset.

If we were to build a notebook to show describe in use against the iris dataset (loaded in the previous example), we would end up with a display like this:

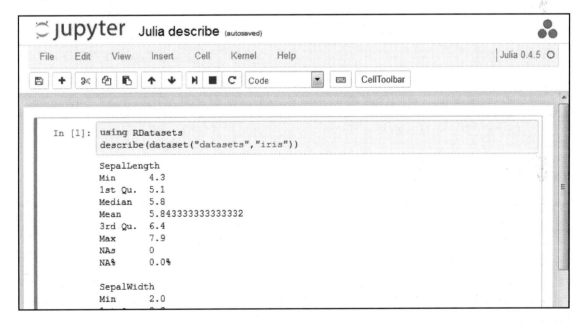

You can see the standard statistics generated for each of the variables in the dataset. I thought it was interesting that the count and percentage of NA values in the dataset are provided. I have found that I usually have to double-check to exclude this data using other languages. Here, it is a quick, built-in reminder.

Julia visualizations in Jupyter

The most popular tool for visualizations in Julia is the `Gadfly` package. We can add the `Gadfly` package (as described at the beginning of this chapter) using the add function:

```
Pkg.add("Gadfly")
```

From then on, we can make reference to the `Gadfly` package in any script using the following command:

```
using Gadfly
```

Julia Gadfly scatterplot

We can use the `plot()` function with standard defaults (no type arguments) to generate a scatterplot. For example, with the simple script:

```
using Gadfly
srand(111)
plot(x=rand(7), y=rand(7))
```

 We use the `srand()` function in all examples that use random results. The `srand()` function sets the random number seed value, so all results in this chapter are reproducible.

We generate a nice, clean scatterplot, as shown in the following screenshot:

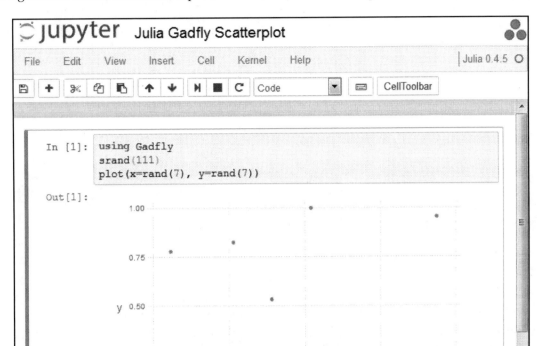

Julia Gadfly histogram

We can produce other graph types as well, for example, a histogram using this script:

```
using Gadfly
srand(111)
plot(x=randn(113), Geom.histogram(bincount=10))
```

This script generates 113 random numbers and generates a histogram of the results.

We see something like the following screenshot:

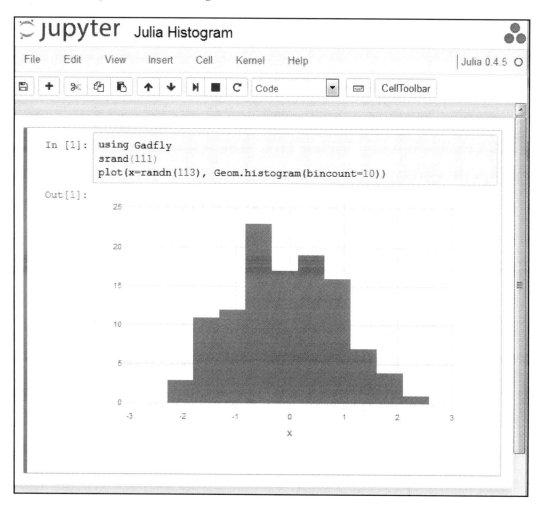

Julia Winston plotting

Another graphics package in Julia is `Winston`. It has similar plotting capabilities to `Gadfly` (I think `Gadfly` is more up-to-date). We can produce a similar plot of random numbers using the following script:

```
using Winston
# fix the random seed so we have reproducible results
srand(111)
```

```
# generate a plot
pl = plot(cumsum(rand(100) .- 0.5), "g", cumsum(rand(100) .- 0.5), "b")
# display the plot
display(pl)
```

Note that, you have to specifically display the plot. The `Winston` package assumes you want to store the graphic as a file, so the `plot` function generates an object for handling.

Moving this into a notebook, we get the following screenshot:

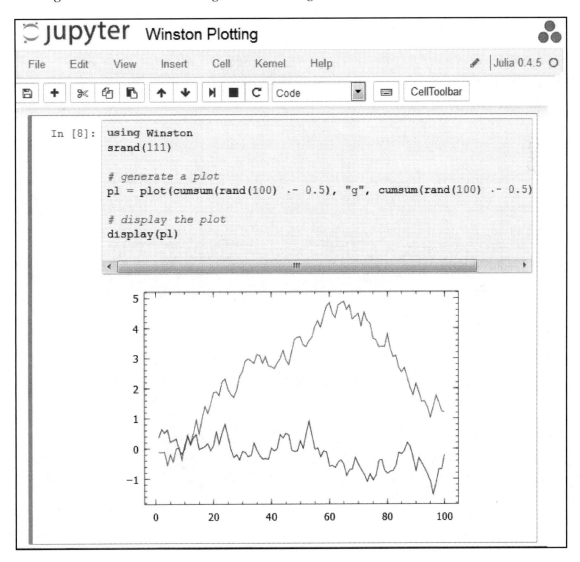

Julia Vega plotting

Another popular graphics package is `Vega`. The main feature of `Vega` is the ability to describe your graphic using language primitives, such as JSON. `Vega` produces most of the standard plots. Here is an example script using `Vega` for a pie chart:

```
#Pkg.add("Vega")
#Pkg.add("Compat")
#Pkg.add("Patchwork")
using Vega
using Compat
using Patchwork
Patchwork.load_js_runtime()
stock = ["chairs", "tables", "desks", "rugs", "lamps"];
quantity = [15, 10, 10, 5, 20];
piechart(x = stock, y = quantity)
```

The generated graphic produced in Jupyter is shown in the following screenshot:

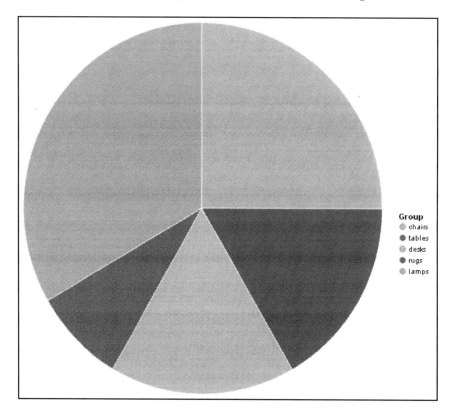

Vega gives you the option on the resultant display to **Save As PNG**.

Julia PyPlot plotting

Another plotting package available is `PyPlot`. `PyPlot` is one of the standard Python visualization libraries and is directly accessible from Julia. We can take this small script to produce an interesting visualization:

```
#Pkg.add("PyPlot")
using PyPlot
precipitation = [0,0,0,0,0,0,0,0,0,0,0.12,0.01,0,0,0,0.37,0,0,0,0,
    0.01,0,0,0,0.01,0.01,0,0.17,0.01,0.11,0.31]
date = collect(1:31)
fig = figure(1, figsize=(4, 4))
plot(date, precipitation, ".")
title("Boston Precipitation")
xlabel("May 2013")
ylabel("Precipitation")
```

The resultant output in Jupyter will look like the following screenshot:

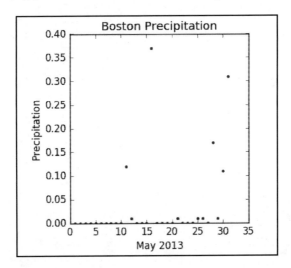

Julia parallel processing

An advanced built-in feature of Julia is to use parallel processing in your script. Normally, you can specify the number of processes that you want to use, directly in Julia. However, in Jupyter, you would use the `addproc()` function to add an additional process available for use in your script. For example, this small script:

```
addprocs(1)
srand(111)
r = remotecall(rand, 2, 3, 4)
s = @spawnat 2 1 .+ fetch(r)
fetch(s)
```

This example makes a call to `rand`, the random number generator with that code executing on the 2nd parameter to the function call (process 2), and then passes the remaining arguments to the `rand` function there (making `rand` generate a 3 x 4 matrix of random numbers). `spawnat` is a macro that evaluates the processes mentioned. Then, `fetch` accesses the result of the spawned processes.

We can see the results in the example in Jupyter as shown in the following screenshot:

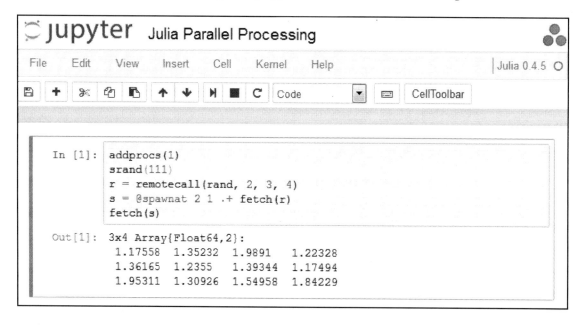

Julia control flow

Julia has a complete set of control flows. As an example, we could have a small function that determines the larger of two numbers:

```
function larger(x, y)
    if (x>y)
        return x
    end
    return y
end
println(larger(7,8))
```

There are several features that you must note:

- The end statement for the if statement
- end the closing of the function
- Indentation of the statements within the function
- Indentation of the handling of a true condition within an if statement

If we run this in Jupyter, we see the output shown in the following screenshot:

```
In [3]:  function larger(x, y)
             if (x>y)
                 return x
             end
             return y
         end
         println(larger(7,8))


         8
```

Julia regular expressions

Julia has built-in regular expression handling–as do most modern programming languages. There is no need for a using statement, as regular expressions are basic features of strings in Julia.

We could have a small script that verifies whether a string matches a phone number, for example:

```
ismatch(r"^\([0-9]{3}\) [0-9]{3}-[0-9]{4}$", "(781)244-1212")
ismatch(r"^\([0-9]{3}\) [0-9]{3}-[0-9]{4}$", "-781-244-1212")
```

When run in Jupyter, we see the following results, that is the first number is conformant to the format and the second is not:

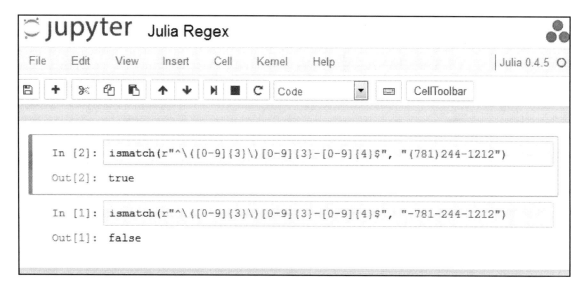

Julia unit testing

As a full language, Julia has unit testing abilities to make sure your code is performing as expected. The unit tests usually reside in the `tests` folder.

Two of the standard functions available for unit testing in Julia are `FactCheck` and `Base.Test`. They both do the same thing, but react differently to failed tests. `FactCheck` will generate an error message that will not stop processing on a failure. If you provide an error handler, that error handler can take control of the test.

`Base.Test` will throw an exception and stop processing on the first test failure. In that regard, it is probably not useful as a unit testing function so much as a runtime test that you may put in place to make sure parameters are within reason, or otherwise, just stop processing before something bad happens.

Both packages are built-in to the standard Julia distributions.

As an example, we can create a `unit tests` notebook that does the same tests and see the resulting, different responses for errors (that is, test failures).

For `FactCheck`, we will use this script:

```
using FactCheck
f(x) = x^3
facts("cubes") do
    @fact f(2) --> 8
    @fact f(2) --> 7
End
```

We are using the `FactCheck` package. The simple function we are testing is cubing a number, but it could be anything. We wrap our tests in a `facts() do...end` block. Each of the tests is run within the block separate from any other block–so as to group our unit tests together–and is prefixed with `@fact`. Also, note we are testing whether the function result following `-->` is the right-hand argument.

When we run this in Jupyter, we see the results shown in the following screenshot:

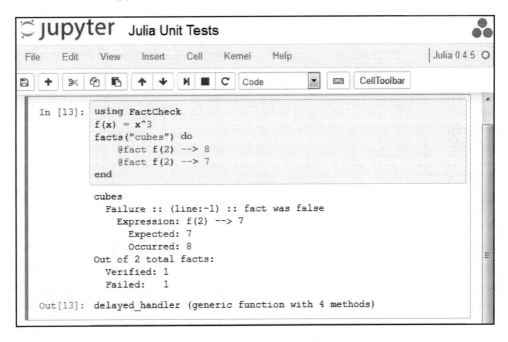

You can see the failed test, why it failed, what line it was on, and so on, as well as the summary of the facts block that was executed, that is, the number of tests that passed (verified) and the number of tests that failed. Note that, the script continued to run onto the next line.

For `Base.Test`, we have a similar script:

```
using Base.Test
f(x) = x^3
@test f(2) == 8
@test f(2) == 7
```

We are using the `Base.Test` package. The function definition we are using is, again, cubing. Then each test is individually–not as part of a test block–prefixed with `@test`. Running this script in Jupyter, we see similar results, as shown in the following screenshot:

```
In [9]:  using Base.Test
         f(x) = x^3
         @test f(2) == 8
         @test f(2) == 7

         LoadError: test failed: 8 == 7
          in expression: f(2) == 7
         while loading In[9], in expression starting on line 4

          in error at error.jl:21
          in default_handler at test.jl:28
          in do_test at test.jl:53
```

The failed test information is displayed. However, in this case, the script stopped executing at this point. Hence, I would only consider this for runtime checks to validate input formats.

Summary

In this chapter, we added the ability to use Julia scripts in your Jupyter Notebook. We added a Julia library not included in the standard Julia installation. We saw basic features of Julia in use. We outlined some of the limitations encountered using Julia in Jupyter. We displayed graphics using some of the graphics packages available, including `Gadfly`, `Winston`, `Vega`, and `PyPlot`. We saw parallel processing in action. We saw a small control flow example, and lastly, we saw how to add unit testing to your Julia script.

In the next chapter, we will learn all about using JavaScript in a Jupyter Notebook.

5
Jupyter JavaScript Coding

JavaScript is a high-level, dynamic, untyped, and interpreted programming language. There are several, languages that are based on JavaScript. In the case of Jupyter, the underlying JavaScript is really Node.js. Node.js is an event-based framework that uses JavaScript that can be used to develop large, scalable applications. Note, this is in contrast to the earlier languages covered in this book that are primarily used for data analysis (Python is a general language as well, but has clear aspects that deal with its capabilities of performing data analysis).

In this chapter, we will cover the following topics:

- Adding JavaScript packages to Jupyter
- JavaScript Hello World Jupyter Notebook
- Basic JavaScript in Jupyter
- Node.js d3 package
- Node.js stats-analysis package
- Node.js JSON handling
- Node.js canvas package
- Node.js plotly package
- Node.js asynchronous threads
- Node.js decision-tree package

Adding JavaScript scripting to your installation

In this section, we will install JavaScript scripting on Mac and Windows. There are separate steps for getting JavaScript scripting available on your Jupyter installation for each environment. The Mac installation was very clean. The Windows installation appears to still be in flux and I would expect the following instructions to change over time.

Adding JavaScript scripts to Jupyter on Mac

Using JavaScript in Jupyter on Mac takes several steps. Jupyter on Mac is also known as **IJavascript**. The definitive site for this is `https://www.npmjs.com/package/ijavascript` specifically earmarked as providing the JavaScript kernel for Jupyter.

On the **Installation** page (`http://n-riesco.github.io/ijavascript/doc/install.md.html`) we can follow the guidelines given for macOS (the current operating system for Mac):

```
ruby -e "$(curl -fsSL
https://raw.githubusercontent.com/Homebrew/install/master/install)"
brew install pkg-config node zeromq
sudo easy_install pip
sudo pip install -U jupyter
npm install ijavascript
```

We can start our notebook with the `ijs` command.

 The command is not available under OSX unless the `-g` option was specified.

You should see a JavaScript notebook available, as shown in the following screenshot:

Adding JavaScript scripts to Jupyter on Windows

There are multiple instructions available on the internet to use JavaScript in Jupyter on Windows. When I originally wrote this chapter I followed one set of instructions that worked. Subsequently, I had made other adjustments to my installation for Jupyter using other languages.

 When I went back to make edits for this chapter and I found the JavaScript implementation is no longer working on Windows. Something along the way disabled and broke the feature. I could not follow the same steps I had taken earlier to enable JavaScript.

I would assume as progress is made on Jupyter that JavaScript will be re-enabled for Jupyter users on Windows.

JavaScript Hello World Jupyter Notebook

Once it's installed, we can attempt the first JavaScript notebook by clicking on the **New** menu and selecting JavaScript. We name the notebook `Hello World Javascript` and put the following lines in this script:

```javascript
var msg = "Hello, World!"
console.log(msg)
```

This script sets a variable and displays the contents of the variable. After entering the script and running (**Cell | Run All**) we end up with a notebook screen that looks like the following screenshot:

We should point out some of the highlights of this page:

- We have the now-familiar language logo in the upper-right that depicts the type of script in use.
- There is output (`Out`) from every line of the notebook. This appears to be a work in progress as line numbering is not meaningful.
- More importantly, we see the true output of the notebook (line 2 in the preceding screenshot) where the string is echoed.
- Otherwise, the notebook looks as familiar to the other types we have seen.

If we look at the contents of the notebook on disk, we see similar results as well:

```
{
  "cells": [
    <<same format as seen earlier for the cells>>
  ],
  "metadata": {
    "kernelspec": {
      "display_name": "Javascript (Node.js)",
      "language": "javascript",
      "name": "javascript"
    },
    "language_info": {
      "file_extension": ".js",
      "mimetype": "application/javascript",
      "name": "javascript",
      "version": "4.2.4"
    }
  },
  "nbformat": 4,
  "nbformat_minor": 0
}
```

So, using the same notebook, in the JSON file format, Jupyter provides a different language for use in the notebook by changing the `metadata` and `language_info` values appropriately.

Adding JavaScript packages to Jupyter

The JavaScript language does not normally install additional packages–it makes reference to other packages via the runtime `include` directive used in your programs. Other packages can be referenced across the network or copied locally into your environment. It is assumed that accessing a library across the network via a CDN is a more efficient and faster mechanism.

However, Node.js adds the `require` verb to the JavaScript syntax. In this case, your code requires another module to be loaded, assumed to be installed in your current environment. To install another module, use npm:

```
npm install name-of-module
```

This would install the module referenced (including any embedded packages that are required) on your machine so that a require statement will work correctly.

Basic JavaScript in Jupyter

JavaScript, and even Node.js, are not usually noted for data handling, but for application (website) development. This differentiates JavaScript coding in Jupyter from the languages covered earlier. But, the examples in this chapter will highlight using JavaScript for application development with data access and analysis features.

JavaScript limitations in Jupyter

JavaScript was originally used specifically to address the need for scripting inside of an HTML page, usually on the client side (in a browser). As such, it was built to be able to manipulate HTML elements on the page. Several packages have been developed to further this feature, even creating a web server, especially using extensions such as Node.js.

The use of any of the HTML manipulation and generation features inside of Jupyter runs into a roadblock since Jupyter expects to control presentation to the user.

Node.js d3 package

The d3 package has data access functionality. In this case, we will read from a tab-separated file and compute an average. Note the use of the underscore variable name for lodash. Variable names starting with an underscore are assumed to be private, although, in this case, it is just a play on the name of the package we are using, lodash, or underscore. Also, lodash is a widely used utility package.

The script we use is as follows:

```
var fs = require("fs");
var d3 = require("d3");
var _ = require("lodash");
//read in the animals file
fs.readFile("data/animals.tsv", "utf8", function(error, data) {
    data = d3.tsv.parse(data);
//display on screen
    console.log(JSON.stringify(data));
//compute the maximum weight
    var maxWeight = d3.max(data, function(d) { return d.avg_weight; });
//display the max on screen
    console.log(maxWeight);
});
```

This assumes we have previously loaded the `fs` and `d3` packages using `npm`, as described in the previous script.

For this example, I created a `data` sub-directory in the same directory my notebook is located (usually the user's home directory) and created a tabbed file (`animal.tsv`) in that directory:

 The use of `<tab>` contains an actual tab character.

```
name<tab>avg_weight
lion<tab>400
tiger<tab>400
human<tab>150
elephant<tab>2000
```

If we load this script into a notebook and run it, we get the following output, as expected:

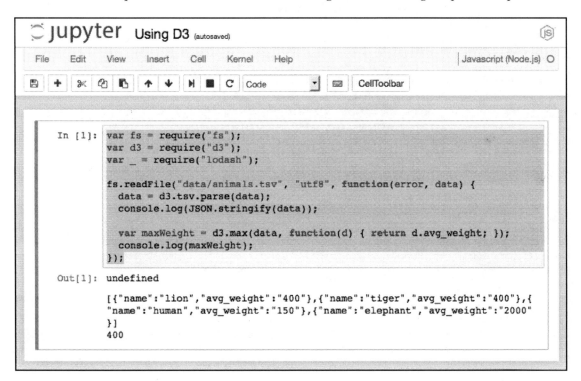

Interestingly, the `max` function does not work as expected. I would have expected that the `2000` pounds of the `elephant` value would be displayed. I have since been informed that if the script property converted the strings to numbers the correct results would have been portrayed.

Node.js stats-analysis package

The `stats-analysis` package has many of the common statistics you may want to perform on your data. You would have to install this package using `npm` as explained previously.

If we had a small set of people's temperatures to work with, we could get some of the statistics on the data readily, using this script:

```
const stats = require("stats-analysis");
var arr = [98, 98.6, 98.4, 98.8, 200, 120, 98.5];
//standard deviation
var my_stddev = stats.stdev(arr).toFixed(2);
//mean
var my_mean = stats.mean(arr).toFixed(2);
//median
var my_median = stats.median(arr);
//median absolute deviation
var my_mad = stats.MAD(arr);
// Get the index locations of the outliers in the data set
var my_outliers = stats.indexOfOutliers(arr);
// Remove the outliers
var my_without_outliers = stats.filterOutliers(arr);
//display our stats
console.log("Raw data is ", arr);
console.log("Standard Deviation is ", my_stddev);
console.log("Mean is ", my_mean);
console.log("Median is ", my_median);
console.log("Median Abs Deviation is " + my_mad);
console.log("The outliers of the data set are ", my_outliers);
console.log("The data set without outliers is ", my_without_outliers);
```

When this script is entered in a notebook we get something similar to the following screenshot:

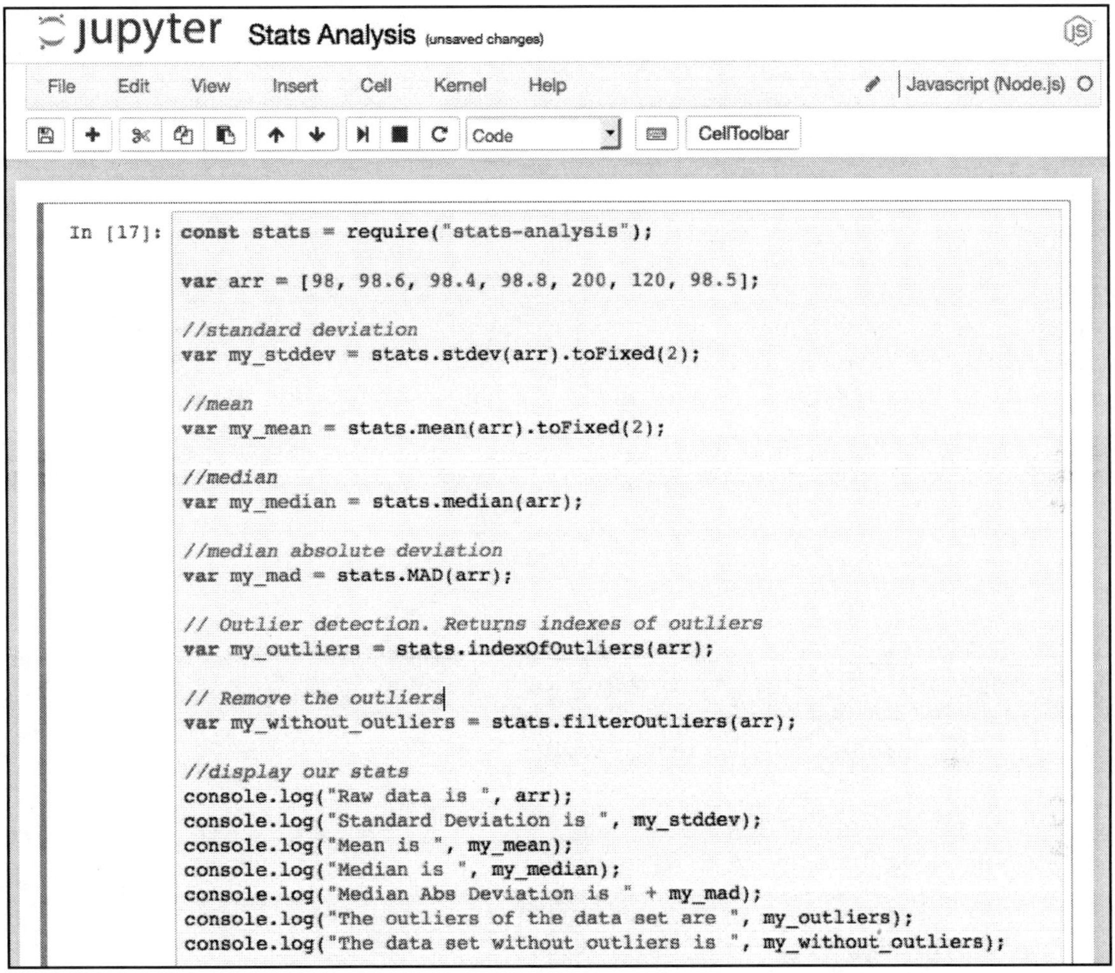

When run, we get the results shown in the following screenshot:

```
Raw data is   [ 98, 98.6, 98.4, 98.8, 200, 120, 98.5 ]
Standard Deviation is   35.07
Mean is   116.04
Median is   98.6
Median Abs Deviation is 0.20000000000000284
The outliers of the data set are   [ 4, 5, 6 ]
The data set without outliers is   [ 98, 98.6, 98.4, 98.8 ]
```

Interestingly, the 98.5 is considered an outlier. I assume there is an optional parameter to the command that would change the limits used. Otherwise, the results are as expected.

The outliers are coming from dealing with the raw data as pure mathematical items. So, from the data provided we have identified the outliers. However, we would probably use a different method to determine outliers, since we know the domain–average human temperatures.

Node.js JSON handling

In this example, we will load a JSON dataset and perform some standard manipulations of the data. I am referencing the list of Ford models from http://www.carqueryapi.com/api /0.3/?callback=?&cmd=getModels&make=ford. I could not reference this directly as it is not a flat file but an API call. So, I downloaded the data into a local file, fords.json. Also, the output from the API call wraps the JSON like ?(jsonï»¿); which would have to be removed before parsing.

The scripting we will use is as follows. In the script, JSON is a built-in package of Node.js so we can reference this package directly. The JSON package provides many of the standard tools that you need to handle your JSON files and objects.

Of interest here is the JSON file reader that constructs a standard JavaScript array of objects. Attributes of each object can be referenced by name, for example, model.model_name. We can see this feature in action with this script that reads in a JSON file and parses out the data elements of interest, based on the field names in the JSON file:

```
//load the JSON dataset
//http://www.carqueryapi.com/api/0.3/
?callback=?&cmd=getModels&make=ford
var fords = require('/Users/dtoomey/fords.json');
//display how many Ford models are in our data set
console.log("There are " + fords.Models.length +
" Ford models in the data set");
//loop over the set
var index = 1
for(var i=0; i<fords.Models.length; i++) {
    //get this model
    var model = fords.Models[i];
    //pull it's name
    var name = model.model_name;
    //if the model name does not have numerics in it
    if(! name.match(/[0-9]/i)) {
        //display the model name
```

```
        console.log("Model " + index + " is a " + name);
        index++;
    }
    //only display the first 5
    if (index>5) break;
}
```

If we pull this script into a new notebook entry, we get the following screen:

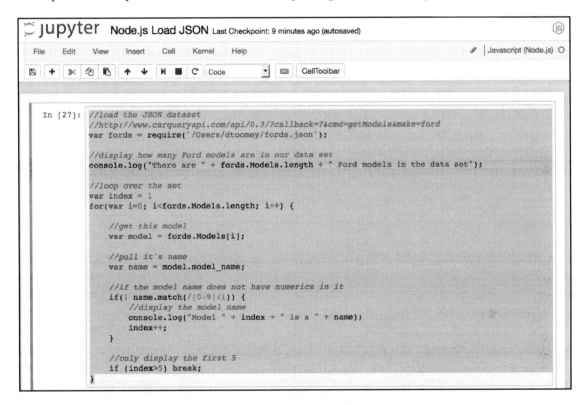

When the lines are executed, we get the expected results, as follows:

```
There are 147 Ford models in the data set
Model 1 is a Aerostar
Model 2 is a Anglia
Model 3 is a Artic
Model 4 is a Aspire
Model 5 is a Bantam

Out[27]: 5
```

Node.js canvas package

The `canvas` package is used for generating graphics in Node.js. We can use the example from the Canvas home page (`https://www.npmjs.com/package/canvas`).

First we need to install `canvas` and its dependencies. There are directions on the home page for the different operating systems, but it is very familiar to the tools we have seen before (we have seen them for macOS):

```
npm install canvas
brew install pkg-config cairo libpng jpeg giflib
```

With the `canvas` package installed on your machine, we can use a small Node.js script to create a graphic:

```javascript
// create a canvas 200 by 200 pixels
var Canvas = require('canvas')
  , Image = Canvas.Image
  , canvas = new Canvas(200, 200)
  , ctx = canvas.getContext('2d')
  , string = "Jupyter!";
// place our string on the canvas
ctx.font = '30px Impact';
ctx.rotate(.1);
ctx.fillText(string, 50, 100);
var te = ctx.measureText(string);
ctx.strokeStyle = 'rgba(0,0,0,0.5)';
ctx.beginPath();
ctx.lineTo(50, 102);
ctx.lineTo(50 + te.width, 102);
ctx.stroke();
//create an html img tag, with embedded graphics
console.log('<img src="' + canvas.toDataURL() + '" />');
```

This script is creating a canvas, writing the string `Jupyter!` across the canvas and then generating an HTML `img` tag with the graphic.

After we run the script in a notebook, we get the `img` tag as the output:

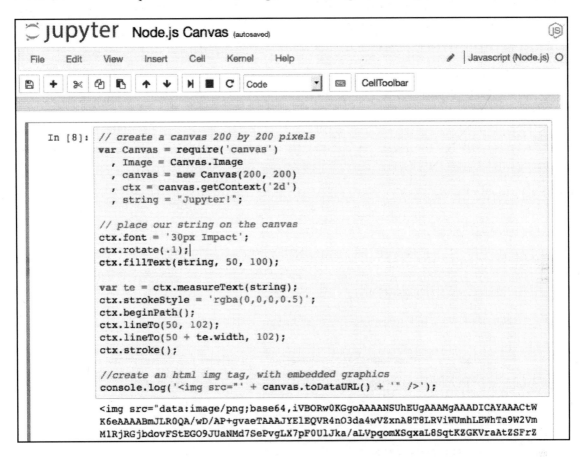

We can take the `img` tag, save it to an HTML page, and then open the HTML file with a browser to display our graphic:

Node.js plotly package

`plotly` is a package that works differently to most. To use their software, you must register with a username and be provided an API key (at `https://plot.ly/`). You then place the username and API key in your script. At that point you can use all of the `plotly` features.

Firstly, like other packages, we need to install it:

```
npm install plotly
```

Once installed, we can reference the `plotly` package as needed. Using a simple script, we can generate a histogram with `plotly`:

```javascript
//set random seed
var seedrandom = require('seedrandom');
var rng = seedrandom('Jupyter');
//setup plotly
var plotly = require('plotly')(username="<username>", api_key="<key>")
var x = [];
for (var i = 0; i < 500; i ++) {
    x[i] = Math.random();
}
require('plotly')(username, api_key);
var data = [
  {
    x: x,
    type: "histogram"
  }
];
var graphOptions = {filename: "basic-histogram", fileopt: "overwrite"};
plotly.plot(data, graphOptions, function (err, msg) {
    console.log(msg);
});
```

Once loaded and run in Jupyter as a notebook, we get the following screenshot:

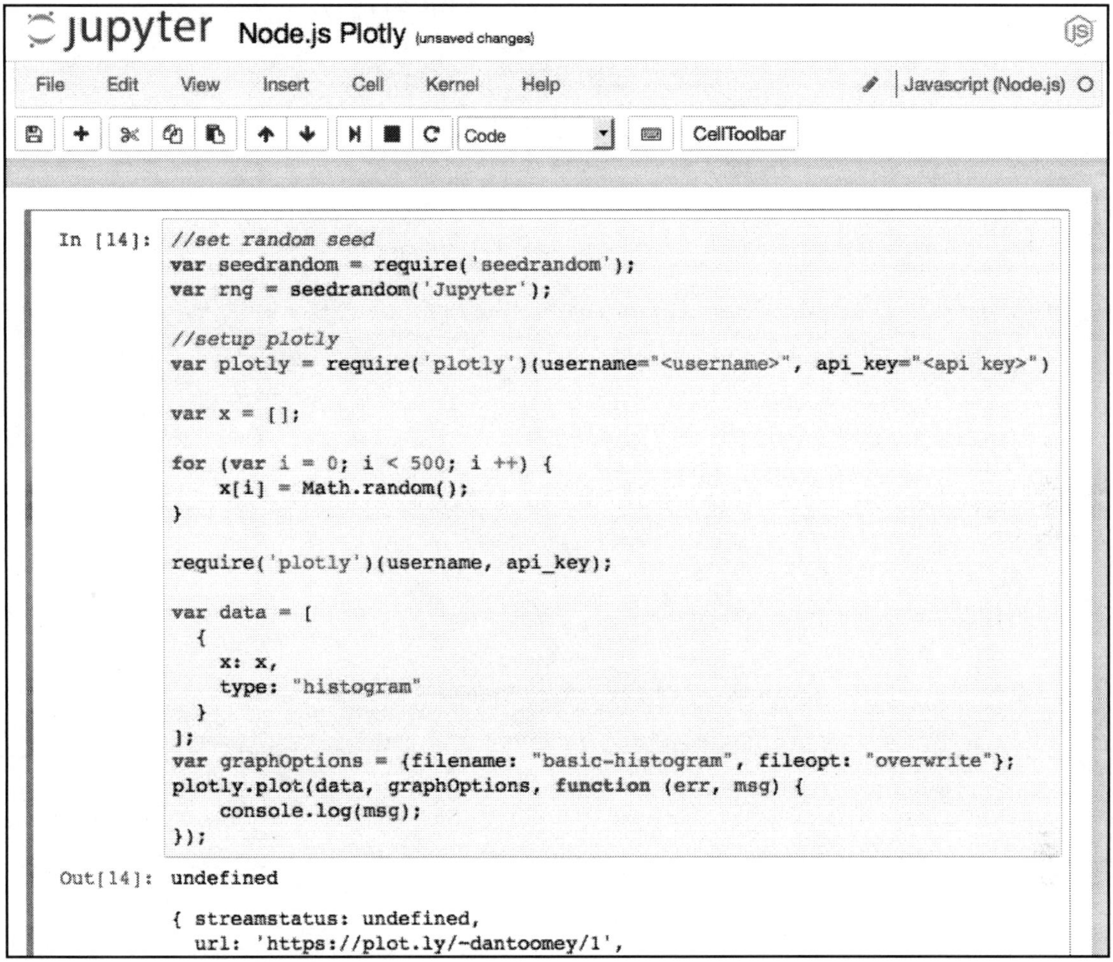

```
⟲ Jupyter  Node.js Plotly (unsaved changes)                                          (JS)

File    Edit    View    Insert    Cell    Kernel    Help           🖉 | Javascript (Node.js) ○

💾  +  ✂  ⧉  📋  ↑  ↓  ▶ ■ C  Code        ▾  |  ▣  CellToolbar


   In [14]:  //set random seed
             var seedrandom = require('seedrandom');
             var rng = seedrandom('Jupyter');

             //setup plotly
             var plotly = require('plotly')(username="<username>", api_key="<api key>")

             var x = [];

             for (var i = 0; i < 500; i ++) {
                 x[i] = Math.random();
             }

             require('plotly')(username, api_key);

             var data = [
               {
                 x: x,
                 type: "histogram"
               }
             ];
             var graphOptions = {filename: "basic-histogram", fileopt: "overwrite"};
             plotly.plot(data, graphOptions, function (err, msg) {
                 console.log(msg);
             });

   Out[14]:  undefined

             { streamstatus: undefined,
               url: 'https://plot.ly/~dantoomey/1',
```

Instead of creating a local file, or just displaying the graphic on screen, any graphic is created and stored on the plotly site and the output of the plot command is a set of return values from your graphic creation. Most important is the URL where you can access the graphic.

So ideally, what should happen is that I should be able to access my graphic (histogram) using the URL provided, which is `https://plot.ly/~dantoomey/1`. The returned URL works as expected, inserting a tilde character in the URL. However, when I looked around the plotly site, I did find my graphics in slightly different paths than expected. All of your graphics are in your home page, for example, `https://plot.ly/~dantoomey`. I can now access all of my graphics and the histogram is shown:

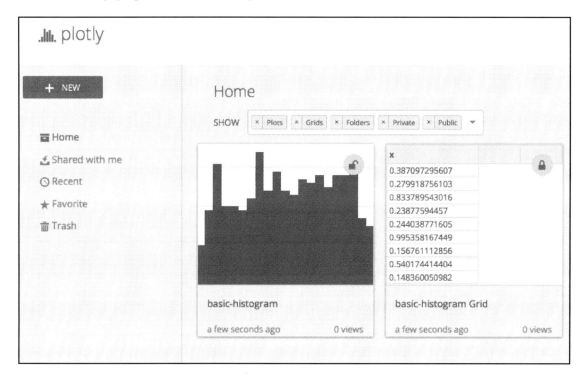

Node.js asynchronous threads

Node.js has built-in mechanisms for creating threads and having them fire asynchronously. Using an example from `http://book.mixu.net/node/ch7.html`, we have the following:

```
//thread function - invoked for every number in items array
function async(arg, callback) {
  console.log('cube ''+arg+'', and return 2 seconds later');
  setTimeout(function() { callback(arg * 3); }, 2000);
}
//function called once - after all threads complete
function final() { console.log('Done', results); }
```

```
//list of numbers to operate upon
var items = [ 0, 1, 1, 2, 3, 5, 7, 11 ];
//results of each step
var results = [];
//loop the drives the whole process
items.forEach(function(item) {
  async(item, function(result){
    results.push(result);
    if(results.length == items.length) {
      final();
    }
  })
});
```

This script creates an asynchronous function that operates on a number. For every number (item), we call upon the inline function passing the number to the function that applies the number to the results list. In this case, it just triples the number and waits for two seconds. The main loop (at the bottom of the script) creates a thread for each number in the list and then waits for them all to complete before calling the `final()` routine.

The notebook page looks like this:

When we run the script, we get something like this output:

```
            triple '0', and return 2 seconds later
            triple '1', and return 2 seconds later
            triple '1', and return 2 seconds later
            triple '2', and return 2 seconds later
            triple '3', and return 2 seconds later
            triple '5', and return 2 seconds later
            triple '7', and return 2 seconds later
            triple '11', and return 2 seconds later

Out[5]:  undefined

            Done [ 0, 3, 3, 6, 9, 15, 21, 33 ]
```

It is odd to see the delay for the last line of output (from the `final()` routine) to display, although we specifically stated to add a delay when we coded the `async` function.

Also, when I played around with other functions, such as cubing each number, the results list came back in a very different order. I would not have thought such a basic math function would have any effect on performance.

Node.js decision-tree package

The `decision-tree` package is an example of a machine learning package. It is available at `https://www.npmjs.com/package/decision-tree`. The package is installed using the following command:

```
npm install decision-tree
```

We need a dataset to use for training/developing our decision tree. I am using the car MPG dataset on this page: `https://alliance.seas.upenn.edu/~cis520/wiki/index.php?n=Lectures.DecisionTrees`. It did not seem to be available directly, so I copied it into Excel and saved it as a local CSV.

The logic for machine learning is very similar:

- Load our dataset
- Split into a training set and a testing set
- Use the training set to develop our model
- Test the mode on the test set.

Typically, you might use two-thirds of your data for training and one-third for testing.

Using the `decision-tree` package and the car MPG dataset we would have a script similar to the following:

```
//Import the modules
var DecisionTree = require('decision-tree');
var fs = require("fs");
var d3 = require("d3");
var util = require('util');
//read in the car/mpg file
fs.readFile("/Users/dtoomey/car-mpg.csv", "utf8", function(error, data)
{
    //parse out the csv into a dataset
    var dataset = d3.tsv.parse(data);
    //display on screen - just for debugging
    //console.log(JSON.stringify(dataset));
    var rows = dataset.length;
    console.log("rows = " + rows);
    var training_size = rows * 2 / 3;
    console.log("training_size = " + training_size);
    var test_size = rows - training_size;
    console.log("test_size = " + test_size);
    //Prepare training dataset
    var training_data = dataset.slice(1, training_size);
    //Prepare test dataset
    var test_data = dataset.slice(training_size, rows);
    //Setup Target Class used for prediction
    var class_name = "mpg";
    //Setup Features to be used by decision tree
    var features = ["cylinders","displacement","horsepower",
    "weight","acceleration", "modelyear", "maker"];
    //Create decision tree and train model
    var dt = new DecisionTree(training_data, class_name, features);
    console.log("Decision Tree is " + util.inspect
    (dt, {showHidden: false, depth: null}));
    //Predict class label for an instance
    var predicted_class = dt.predict({
        cylinders: 8,
        displacement: 400,
        horsepower: 200,
        weight: 4000,
        acceleration: 12,
        modelyear: 70,
```

```
        maker: "US"
});
console.log("Predicted Class is " + util.inspect
(predicted_class, {showHidden: false, depth: null}));
//Evaluate model on a dataset
var accuracy = dt.evaluate(test_data);
console.log("Accuracy is " + accuracy);
//Export underlying model for visualization or inspection
var treeModel = dt.toJSON();
console.log("Decision Tree JSON is " +
util.inspect(treeModel, {showHidden: false, depth: null}));
});
```

There is wide use of console.log to display progressive information about the processing that is occurring. I am using the util() function further, to display members of objects in use.

 The packages must also be installed using npm.

If we run this in a notebook, we end up with the results shown in the following screenshot:

```
Out[23]: undefined

    rows = 42
    training_size = 28
    test_size = 14
    Decision Tree is { data:
        [ { 'mpg,cylinders,displacement,horsepower,weight,acceleration,modelye
    ar,maker': 'Bad,8,400,170,4746,12,71,America' },
            { 'mpg,cylinders,displacement,horsepower,weight,acceleration,modelye
```

We arrive at a model for determining whether the MPG for a vehicle is acceptable or not, based on the vehicle characteristics. In this case, we have a *bad* predictor as noted in the results.

Summary

In this chapter, we learned how to add JavaScript to our Jupyter Notebook. We saw some of the limitations of using JavaScript in Jupyter. We had a look at examples of several packages that are typical of Node.js coding, including d3 for graphics, stats-analysis for statistics, built-in JSON handling, canvas for creating graphics files, and plotly used for generating graphics with a third party tool. We also saw how multi-threaded applications can be developed using Node.JS under Jupyter. Lastly, we saw how to use machine learning to develop a decision tree.

In the next chapter, we will see how to create interactive widgets that can be used in your notebook.

6
Interactive Widgets

There is a mechanism built for Jupyter to gather input from the user as the script is running. To do this, we put in coding in the form of a *widget* or user interface control in the script. The widgets we will use in this chapter are defined at `http://ipywidgets.readthedocs.io/en/latest/`.

There are widgets for the following:

- **Text input**: Notebook users enter a string that will be used later in the script.
- **Button clicks**: The user is presented with multiple options in the form of buttons; then, depending on which button is selected (clicked on), your script can change direction according to the user.
- **Slider**: You can provide the user with a *slider* with which the user can select a value within the range you specify, and then your script can use that value accordingly.
- **Toggle box and checkboxes**: The user selects the different options of your script that they are interested in working with.
- **Progress bar**: If your script will take some time to process, it would be considerate to present a progress bar so they have some idea of how long it might take to finish. Similarly, a progress bar can be used to show how far along they are in a multi-step process.
- There are a few constraints to the types of input you can gather from the user. So, you could make really interesting widgets that do not fit the standard user input control paradigm. For example, there is a widget (`ipyleaflet`) allowing a user to click on a geographical map where the underlying script will get the geographic data point selected and operate accordingly.

In this chapter, we will cover the following topics:

- Installing widgets
- Widget basics
- Interact widget
- Interactive widget
- Widgets package

Installing widgets

The widgets package is an upgrade to the standard Jupyter installation. You can update the widgets package using this command:

```
pip install ipywidgets
```

Note that, if `ipywidgets` is already installed on your machine you may need to use this command for the upgrade to take effect:

```
pip install â??upgrade ipywidgets
```

Once complete, you must then upgrade your Jupyter installation using this command:

```
jupyter nbextension enable --py widgetsnbextension
```

You may have to restart your notebook for the extensions to take effect.

If you do not install the package and the upgrade, then when you run your widgets script you will get a warning message in the displayâ??**The installed widget JavaScript is the wrong version**:

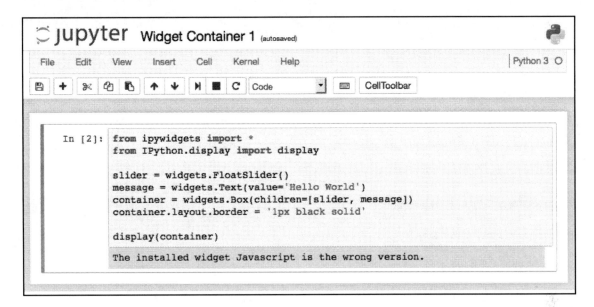

 I updated my installation, but still received the warning message for some screens. I assume it is a matter of time before this warning message bug is resolved in a future version of the software.

Widget basics

All widgets work the same, generally:

- You create or define an instance of a widget.
- You can preset attributes of a widget, such as its initial value or a label to be displayed.
- Widgets can react to different inputs from a user. The inputs are gathered by a handler or a Python function that is invoked when a user performs some action on a widget; for example, a function could be set up to call the handler if the user clicks on a button.
- The value of a widget can be used later in your script in the same way as any other variable; for example, you could use a widget to determine how many circles to draw.

Interact widget

Interact is the basic widget that is often used to derive all other widgets. It has variable arguments, and, depending on these arguments, can affect many different variations of user input control.

Interact widget slider

We can use interact to produce a slider by passing in an extent. Take the following script:

```
from ipywidgets import interact
# define a function to work with (cubes the number)
def myfunction(arg):
    return arg+1
interact(myfunction, arg=9);
```

Here, we have a script that does the following:

- References the package we want to use
- Defines a function (which is called for every user input of a value)
- Calls out to interact, passing our *handler* and a range of values

When we run this script, we get a scrollbar that is modifiable by the user:

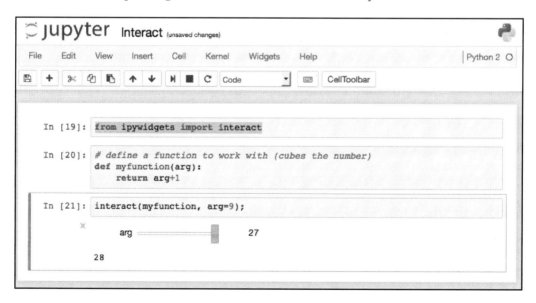

The user is able to *slide* the vertical bar over the range of values. The upper end is **27** and the lower end is **-9** (assume we could pass additional arguments to interact to set the range of values that are selectable). `myfunction` is called every time the value in the `interact` widget is changed and the result printed. As a result, we see **27** selected and the number **28** displayed below the slider (following the processing of `myfunction -27 +1`).

Interact widget checkbox

We can change the type of control generated based on the arguments passed to interact. Take the following script:

```
from ipywidgets import interact
def myfunction(x):
    return x
interact(myfunction, x=False);
```

We are going through the same steps as before; however, the value passed is `False` (could also be `True`). The `interact` function examines the argument passed, determines that it is a Boolean value, and presents the appropriate control for a Boolean–a checkbox:

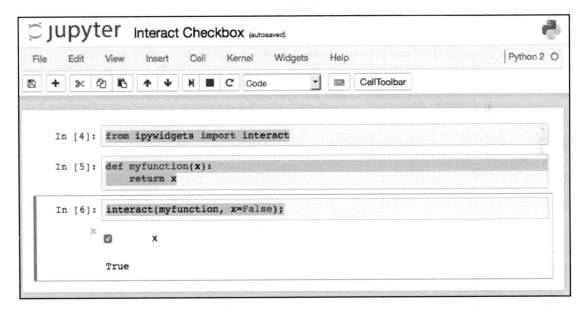

Interact widget text box

We can generate a text input control again by passing in different arguments to `interact`. For example, take the following script:

```
from ipywidgets import interact
def myfunction(x):
    return x
interact(myfunction, x= "Hello World ");
```

The script produces a text input control with the initial value of `"Hello World"`:

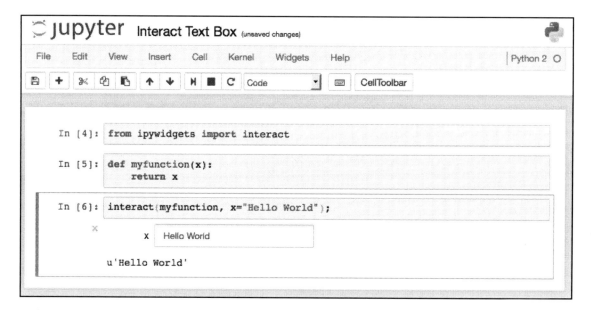

Interact dropdown

We can also use the interactï»¿ï»¿ function to produce a drop-down list box for the user to select from. In the following script, we produce a dropdown with two choices:

```
from ipywidgets import interact
def myfunction(x):
    return x
interact(myfunction, x=('red','green'));
```

This script does the following:

- Pulls in the interact reference
- Defines a function that will be called whenever the user changes the value of the control
- Calls interact with a set of values–interact will interpret this to mean create a dropdown for the user to select from.

If we run this script in a notebook, we get a display like the following:

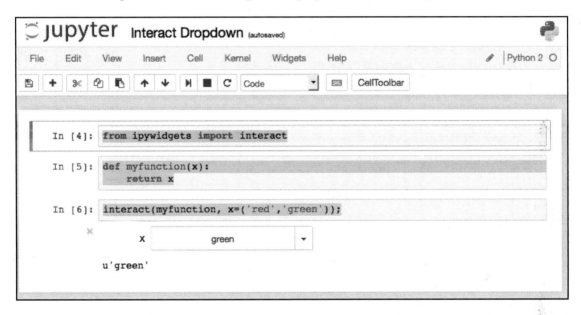

The value printed at the bottom will change according to what is selected in the dropdown by the user.

Interactive widget

There is also an **interactive** widget. The interactive widget works like the interact widget, but does not display the user input control until called upon directly by the script. This would be useful if you had some calculations that had to be performed for the parameters of the widget display, or even if you wanted to decide whether you needed a control at runtime.

For example, we could have the following script (similar to the preceding script):

```
from ipywidgets import interactive
def myfunction(x):
    return x
w = interactive(myfunction, x= "Hello World ");
from IPython.display import display
display(w)
```

There are a couple of changes to the script:

- We are referencing the interactive widget
- The `interactive` function returns a widget, rather than immediately displaying a value
- We must script the display of the widget ourselves

If we run this script, it looks very similar to the result of the previous script:

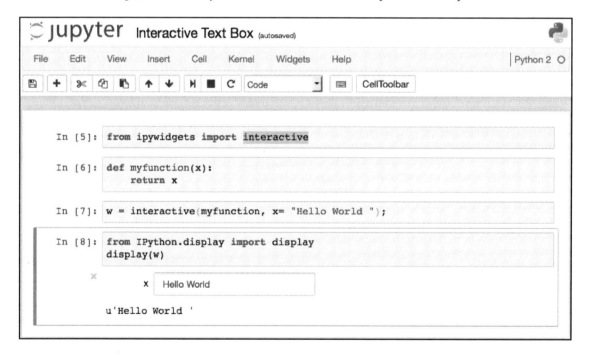

Widgets

There is another package of widgets, called **ipywidgets**, that has all of the standard controls that you might want to use, with many optional parameters available to customize your display.

Progress bar widget

One of the widgets available in this package displays a progress bar to the user. Take the following script:

```
import ipywidgets as widgets
widgets.FloatProgress(
    value=45,
    min=0,
    max=100,
    step=5,
    description='Percent:',
)
```

This would display our progress bar as shown here:

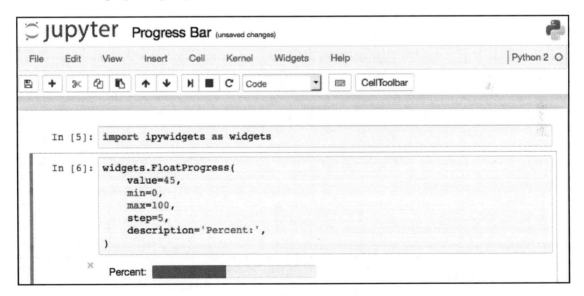

Listbox widget

We could also use the list box widget, called as `Dropdown`, in this script:

```
import ipywidgets as widgets
from IPython.display import display
w = widgets.Dropdown(
    options={'Pen': 7732, 'Pencil': 102, 'Pad': 33331},
    description='Item:',
)
display(w)
w.value
```

This script will display a list box to the user with the displayed values of `Pen`, `Pencil`, and `Pad`. When the user selects one of the values, the associated value is returned to the `w` variable, which we display:

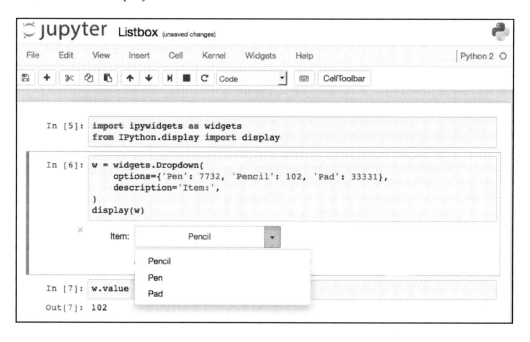

Text widget

The text widget gathers a text string from the user for reuse elsewhere in your script. A text widget has a description (label) and a value (entered by the user, or preset in your script).

In this example we will just gather a text string and display it on screen as part of the output for the script. We will use the following script:

```
from ipywidgets import widgets
from IPython.display import display
text.on_submit(handle_submit)
display(text)
def handle_submit(sender):
    print(text.value)
text.on_submit(handle_submit)
```

The Python package that contains the basic widgets is `ipywidgets`, so we need to reference that. We define a handler for the text field that will be called when the user clicks on **Submit** (after entering their text value). We are using the `Text` widget:

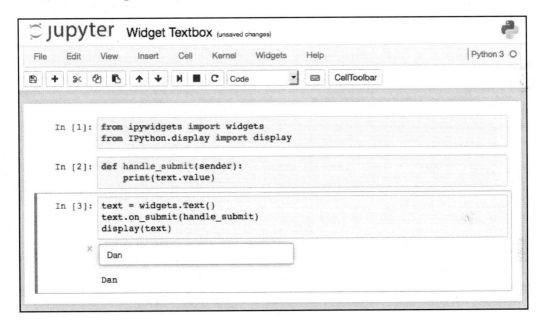

We should point out some of the highlights of this page:

- The ordering of the elements of the page is not important. The page is driven by the `text = ...` statements near the top of the page, where they might appear.
- When invoking a widget, the widget automatically looks for any handlers that might be associated in the script. In this case, we have a `submit` handler. There are many other handlers available. The `text.on_submit` assigns the handler to the widget.
- If no handlers are available, we have a standard Python notebook.

If we run the script (**Cell | Run All**) we get the following screen (waiting for us to enter a value in the textbox):

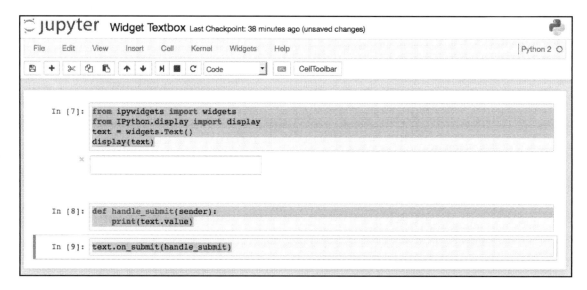

Once we enter a value and hit the Enter key, the script progresses and we have the following output:

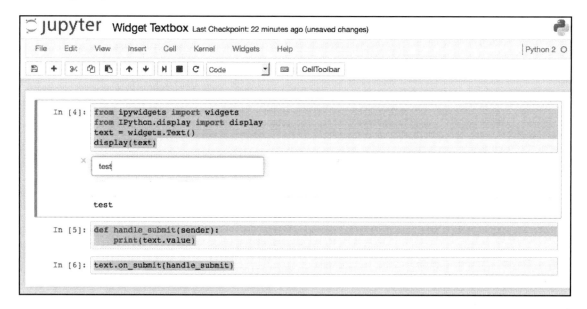

So, our script has set up a widget for gathering input from the user and then, later, has done something with that value (we are just displaying here, but we could use the input for further processing). In the example, I entered the word test into the widget and hit *Enter*. This caused the script to invoke the on_submit handler which printed out the value typed into the field.

Button widget

Similarly, we can use a button widget in our script. For example, take the following script:

```
from ipywidgets import widgets
from IPython.display import display
button = widgets.Button(description="Submit");
display(button)
def on_button_clicked(widget):
    print("Clicked Button:" + widget.description);
button.on_click(on_button_clicked);
```

This script does the following:

- References the features we want to use from the widgets packages.
- Creates our button.
- Defines a handler for the click event on a button. The handler receives the button object that was clicked upon (widget).
- In the handler, we display information about the button clicked on (you can imagine that if we had several buttons in a display, we would want to determine which button was clicked).

- Lastly, it assigns the defined handler to the button object we created.

 The indentation of the coding for the handlerâ⊚⊚this is the standard Python style that must be followed.

If we run this script in a notebook, we get a display like the following:

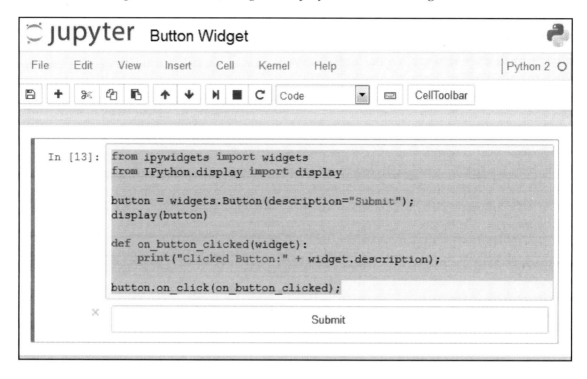

Note the **Submit** button at the bottom of the screenshot. You could change other attributes of the button, such as its position, size, color, and so on.

If we then click on the **Submit** button, we get a display like the following:

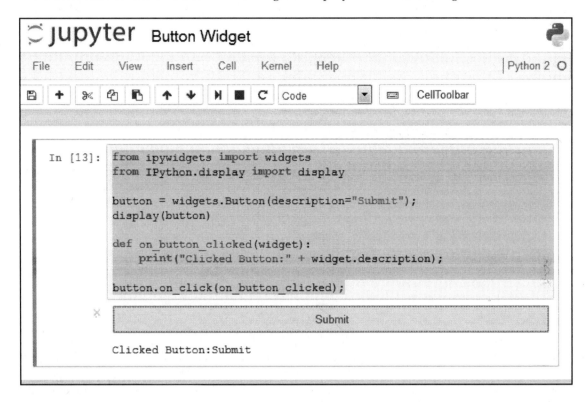

Our message about the button clicked is now displayed.

Widget properties

All of the widgets' controls have a set of properties that can be adjusted as needed for your display. You can see the list of properties by taking an instance of a control and running the `control.keys` command in a notebook. For example, look at the following script:

```
from ipywidgets import *
w = IntSlider()
w.keys
```

This script pulls in a blanket reference to all of the controls available in widgets. We then create an `IntSlider` instance and display the possible list of properties that we can adjust:

```
Out[1]: ['_view_name',
         'orientation',
         'color',
         '_view_module',
         'height',
         'disabled',
         'visible',
         'border_radius',
         'border_width',
         '_model_module',
         'font_style',
         'layout',
         'min',
         '_range',
         'background_color',
         'slider_color',
         'width',
         'continuous_update',
         'font_family',
         '_dom_classes',
         'description',
         '_model_name',
         'max',
         'border_color',
         'readout',
         'padding',
         'font_weight',
         'step',
         'border_style',
         'font_size',
         'msg_throttle',
         'value',
         'margin']
```

As you can see, the list is extensive. The following table shows the list in more detail:

Property	Description
orientation	Whether left-aligned, right-aligned, or justified
color	Color of font
height	Height of control
disabled	Whether control is disabled or not
visible	Is the control displayed?
font_style	Style of font, for example, italics
min	Minimum value (used in range list)
background_color	Background color of control
width	Width of control
font_family	Font family to be used for text in control
description	The description field is used for documentation purposes
max	Maximum value (of range)
padding	Padding applied (to edges of control)
font_weight	Weight of font used in control, for example, bold
font_size	Size of font used for text in control
value	Selected, entered value for control
margin	Margin to use when displaying control

We could adjust any of these in our scripts using something like the following sample script where we disable a text box (the text box will display, but the user cannot enter a value into the text box):

```
from ipywidgets import *
Text(value='You can not change this text!', disabled=True)
```

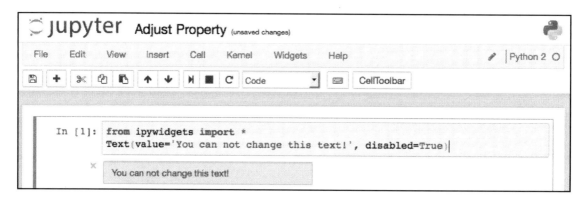

When a field is disabled, the textbox is grayed out, and when the user hovers the cursor over the field they get a red circle with a slash through it, meaning it cannot be changed.

Adjusting properties

All of the properties shown previously are accessible to read and write. We can show this transition with a small script:

```
from ipywidgets import *
w = IntSlider()
original = w.value
w.value = 5
original, w.value
```

The script creates a slider, retrieves its current value, changes the value to 5, and then displays the original and current value of the control.

If we were to run this script in a notebook, we would see the following results:

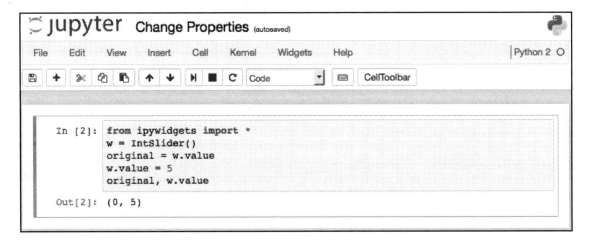

Widget events

All of the controls work by reacting to user actions, either with a mouse or keyboard. The default actions for controls are built into the software, but you can add your own handling of events (user actions).

We have seen this kind of event handling earlier–for example, in the section on the slider, a function is called whenever the slider value is changed by the userâ⊙⊙but let's explore it in a little more depth. We could have the following script:

```python
from ipywidgets import widgets
from IPython.display import display
button = widgets.Button(description="Click Me!")
display(button)
def on_button_clicked(b):
    print("Button clicked.")
button.on_click(on_button_clicked)
```

This script does the following:

- Creates a button.
- Displays the button (to the user).
- Defines handler click events. It prints a message that you clicked on screen. You can have any Python statements in the handler.

- Lastly, it associates the click handler with the button we created. So, now, when the user clicks on our button, the handler is called and the `Button clicked` message is displayed on screen (as shown in the following screenshot).

If we run this script in a notebook and click on the button a few times, we get the following display:

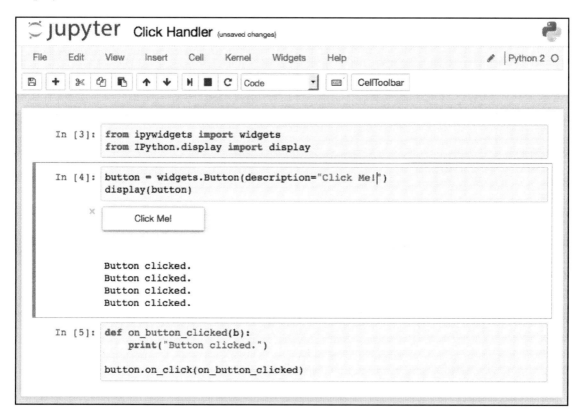

Widget containers

You can also assemble containers of widgets directly using Python syntax by passing the child elements in the constructor. For example, we could have the following script:

```python
from ipywidgets import *
from IPython.display import display
slider = widgets.FloatSlider()
message = widgets.Text(value='Hello World')
container = widgets.Box(children=[slider, message])
```

```
container.layout.border = '1px black solid'
display(container)
```

Here, we are creating a container (which is a box widget) where we are specifying the children contained controls. The call to display the container will iteratively display the child elements as well. So, we end up with a display like the following:

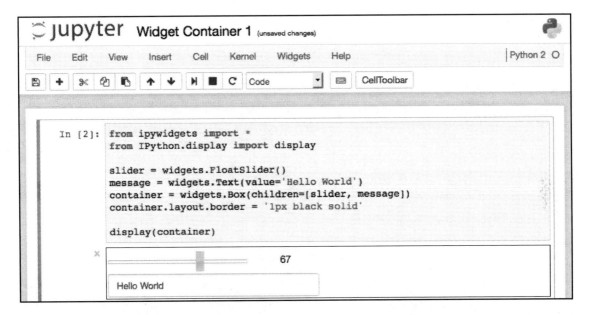

You can see the border around the box and the two controls in the box.

Similarly, we could have added the children to the container after the container was displayed by using syntax like this:

```
from ipywidgets import *
from IPython.display import display
container = widgets.Box()
container.layout.border = '1px black solid'
display(container)
slider = widgets.FloatSlider()
message = widgets.Text(value='Hello World')
container.children=[slider, message]
```

When we add the child to the container, the container repaints, which will cause a repaint of any children.

If we run this script in another notebook, we get a very similar result to the previous example:

Summary

In this chapter, we added widgets to our Jupyter installation and used the interact and interactive widgets to produce a variety of user input controls. We then looked in the widgets package in depth to examine some of the user controls available, the properties available in the containers, the events that are available emitting from the controls, and to work out how to build containers of controls.

In the next chapter, we will learn about sharing notebooks with other users. The typical method for sharing a notebook is to post it on a website so anyone can access the notebook. We will also cover how to convert notebooks to different formats. This allows users who don't have direct access to your notebook to see the effects.

Sharing and Converting Jupyter Notebooks

Once you have developed your notebook, you will want to share it with others. There is a typical mechanism available for sharing that we will cover in this chapter–placing your notebook on an accessible server on the Internet.

When you provide a notebook to another person, they may need the notebook in a different format given their system requirements. We will also cover some mechanisms available for providing your notebook to others in a different format as well.

In this chapter, we will cover the following topics:

- Sharing notebooks
- Converting notebooks

Sharing notebooks

The typical mechanism for sharing notebooks is to provide your notebook on a website. A website runs on a server or on allocated machine space. The server takes care of all the bookkeeping involved in running a website, such as keeping track of multiple users and logging people on and off.

In order for the notebook to be of use, though, the website must have notebook logic installed. A typical website knows how to deliver content as HTML given some source files. The most basic form is pure HTML, where every page you access on the website corresponds exactly to one HTML file on the web server. Other languages could be used to develop the website (such as Java or PHP), so then the server needs to know how to access the HTML it needs from those source files. In our context, the server needs to know how to access your notebook in order to deliver HTML to users.

Even when notebooks are just running on your local machine, they are running in a browser that is accessing your local machine (server) instead of the Internet–so the Web, HTML, and Internet access has already been provided.

If a notebook is on true website, it is available to everyone who can access that website–whether the server is running on your machine in an office environment accessible over the local area network or if your website is available to all users over the Internet.

You can always add security around the website so that the only people who can use your notebook are given access by you. Security mechanisms depend on the type of web server software involved.

Sharing notebooks on a notebook server

Built into the Jupyter process is the ability to expose the notebook as its own web server. Assuming the server is a machine accessible by other users, you can configure Jupyter to run on that server. You must provide the configuration information to Jupyter so it knows how to proceed. The command to generate a configuration file for your Jupyter installation is as follows:

```
jupyter notebook --generate-config
```

This command will generate a `jupyter_notebook_config.py` file in your `~./jupyter` directory. For Microsoft users, that directory is a subdirectory of your home user directory.

The configuration file contains the settings that you can use to expose your notebook as a server:

```
c.NotebookApp.certfile = u'/path/to/your/cert/cert.pem'
c.NotebookApp.keyfile = u'/ path/to/your/cert/key.key'
c.NotebookApp.ip = '*'
c.NotebookApp.password = u'hashed-password'
c.NotebookApp.open_browser = False
c.NotebookApp.port = 8888
```

The settings in the file are explained in this table:

Setting	Description
`c.NotebookApp.certfile`	This is the path to the location of the certificate for your site. If you have an SSL certificate, you will need to change the setting to the location of the file. It may not be a PEM extension file. There are several SSL certificate formats.
`c.NotebookApp.keyfile`	This is the path to the location of the key to access the `cert` for your site. Rather than specify the key to your certificate, you would have stored the key in a file. So, if you want to apply an SSL certificate to your notebook, you need to specify the file location. The key is normally a very large, hexadecimal number. So, it is stored in its own file. Also, storing in a file offers additional protection, as the directory where keys are stored on a machine usually has limited access.
`c.NotebookApp.ip`	This is the IP address of the machine. Use the wildcard `'*'` to open to all. Here, we are specifying the IP address of the machine where the notebook website is accessed.
`c.NotebookApp.password`	Hashed password–the password will have to be provided by users accessing your notebook in response to a standard login challenge.
`c.NotebookApp.open_browser`	`True/False`–does starting the notebook server open a browser window?
`c.NotebookApp.port`	Port to access your server–it should be open to the machine.

Every website is addressed at the lower levels by an IP address. An IP address is a four-part number that identifies the locale of the server involved. An IP address might look like `172.32.88.7`. Web browsers in concert with Internet software know how to use the IP address to locate the server of interest. The set of software also knows how to translate the URL you mentioned in your browser, such as `http://www.microsoft.com`, into an IP address.

Note that, the example configuration provided is not enterprise ready. You need to coordinate with your security personnel to configure correctly. Once you have changed the settings appropriately, you should be able to point a browser at the URL configured and access your notebook. The URL would be the concatenation of either HTTP or HTTPS (depending on whether you applied an SSL certificate), the IP address, and the port, for example, `HTTPS://123.45.56.9:8888`.

Encrypted sharing notebooks on a notebook server

Two of the preceding settings can be used if you have an SSL certificate to apply. Without the SSL certificate, the password (refer to the previous section) and all other interactions will be transmitted from the user's browser to the server in the clear. If you are dealing with sensitive information in your notebook, you should obtain an SSL certificate and make the appropriate settings changes for your server.

If you need more security for access to your notebook, the next step would be to provide an SSL certificate (placed on your machine and the path provided in the configuration file). There are a number of companies that provide SSL certificates. The cheapest at the time of writing is Let's Encrypt, which will provide a low-level SSL certificate for free. (There are gradations of SSL certificates that are not free.)

Again, once you have set the preceding settings with regard to your certificate, you should be able to access your notebook server using the `https://` prefix–knowing that all the transmissions between the user's browser and the notebook server are encrypted and therefore secure. You may need to add your certificate to the keychain on the host machine before browser authentication will work.

Sharing notebooks on a web server

In order to add your notebook to an existing web server, you need to take the preceding steps and add a little more information to the notebook configuration file:

```
c.NotebookApp.tornado_settings = {
    'headers': {
        'Content-Security-Policy': "frame-ancestors
'https://yourwebsite.com' 'self' "
    }
}
```

Here, you replace yourwebsite.com with the URL of your website.

Once complete, you can access the notebook through your website.

Sharing notebooks through Docker

Docker is an open lightweight container for distributing software. A typical Docker instance has an entire web server and a specific web application running on a port in a machine. The specifics about the software running in a Docker instance are governed by the Dockerfile file. This file provides commands to the Docker environment regarding which components to use to configure this instance. Sample Dockerfile contents for a Jupyter implementation are as follows:

```
ENV TINI_VERSION v0.6.0
ADD https://github.com/krallin/tini/releases/download/${TINI_VERSION}/tini
/usr/bin/tini
RUN chmod +x /usr/bin/tini
ENTRYPOINT ["/usr/bin/tini", "--"]
EXPOSE 8888
CMD ["jupyter", "notebook", "--port=8888", "--no-browser", "--ip=0.0.0.0"]
```

Here is a discussion about each of the commands in the `Dockerfile`:

- The `ENV` command tells Docker to use a specialized operating system. This is necessary to overcome a deficiency of Jupyter that keeps obtaining and releasing resources from your machine. TINI is third-party software that provides a minimum Docker initialization.
- The `ADD` command tells Docker where the `tini` code is located.
- The `RUN` command is changing the access rights to the `tini` directory.
- The `ENTRYPOINT` command tells Docker what to use as the operating system of the Docker instance.
- The `EXPOSE` command tells Docker which port to expose your notebook on.
- The `CMD` command tells Docker which commands to run (once the environment is set up).
- Once the Docker instance is deployed to your Docker machine, you can access the Docker instance on the machine at the port specified (8888), for example, `http://machinename.com:8888`.

The instructions mentioned previously assume you are new to Docker. If you have an existing Docker installation the Dockerfile configuration and access to your Jupyter instance in Docker, the instructions would probably change.

Sharing notebooks on a public server

Currently, one of the hosting companies that allows you to host your notebook(s) for free is GitHub. GitHub is the standard web provider of source control (Git source control) systems. Source control is used to maintain historical versions of your files to allow you to retrace your steps. Other hosts include NBViewer, Anaconda, and Wakari.

GitHub's implementation includes all of the tools that you need to use in your notebook already installed on the server. For example, in prior chapters, to use R programming in your notebook you would have had to install the R tool set on your machine. GitHub has already done all of these steps.

In order to host your notebook on GitHub, go to `https://github.com/` and sign up for a free website.

Once logged in, you are provided with a website that can be added to. If you have development tools to use (`git push` commands are programmer commands to store files on a Git server), you can do that or simply drag and drop your notebook (IPYNB) file onto your GitHub website.

I created an account there with a `notebooks` directory, and placed one of the notebooks on that site. My GitHub site looks like this:

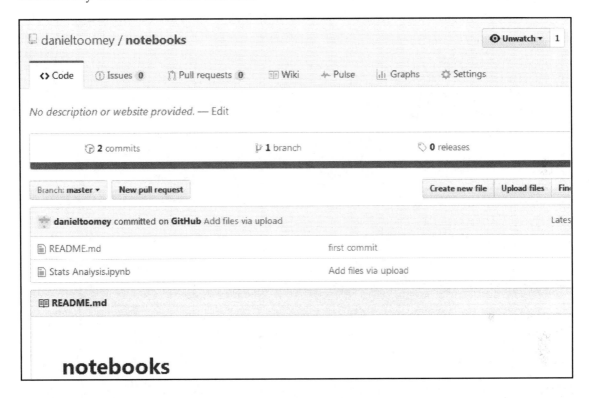

You can see the `Stats Analysis.ipynb` file near the bottom of the screen.

If you click on that notebook file, you see the expected notebook up and running in your browser:

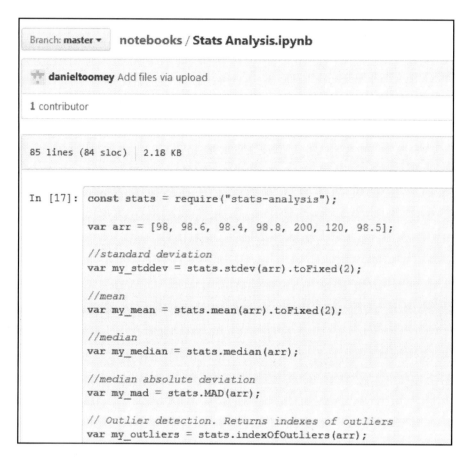

If you look back to this chapter, you can see the same display (less the GitHub adornments).

This notebook is directly accessible by others using the URL `https://github.com/danielt oomey/notebooks/blob/master/Stats%20Analysis.ipynb`. So, you can provide your notebook on GitHub to other users and just hand them the URL.

You are logged into GitHub, so the display will look slightly different as you will have more control over GitHub's contents.

Converting notebooks

The standard tool for converting notebooks to other formats is the `nbconvert` utility. It is built-in to your Jupyter installation. You can access the tool directly in the user interface for your notebook. If you open a notebook, select the Jupyter **File** menu item, and you will see several options for **Download as**:

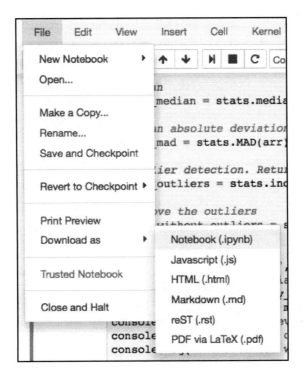

The choices are as follows:

Format type	File extension
Notebook	`.ipynb`
JavaScript	`.js`
HTML	`.html`
Markdown	`.md`
Restructured text	`.rst`
PDF	`.pdf`

For these examples, if we take a notebook from a previous chapter, the Jupyter Notebook looks like this:

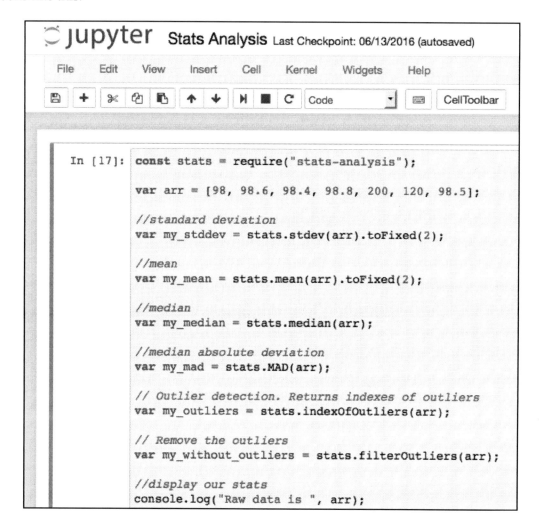

Notebook format

The notebook format (IPYNB) is the native format for your notebook. We have looked into this IPYNB file in earlier chapters to see what Jupyter is storing for your notebook.

You would use the notebook format if you wanted to give another user complete access to your notebook since they would run your notebook from their system.

You may also want to do this to save your notebook in another medium.

JavaScript format

JavaScript (.js) format corresponds to the JavaScript implementation of your notebook. If you used JavaScript as the language for your notebook, this is a direct export of the notebook page.

If you used another language for the script of the notebook, such as Python, then the **Download as** option would change appropriately, that is, **Download as** | **Python(.py)**.

Using our example, as expected, the JS format is equivalent to the Jupyter display:

```
const stats = require("stats-analysis");
var arr = [98, 98.6, 98.4, 98.8, 200, 120, 98.5]
//standard deviation
var my_stddev = stats.stdev(arr).toFixed(2);
//mean
var my_mean = stats.mean(arr).toFixed(2);
//median
var my_median = stats.median(arr);
//median absolute deviation
var my_mad = stats.MAD(arr);
// Outlier detection. Returns indexes of outliers
var my_outliers = stats.indexOfOutliers(arr);
...
```

With the JS format, you can run the script directly using a JavaScript interpreter. On a Mac, there is the `js` command. Similar tools exist for Windows machines.

Also, for other script languages, you should be able to run the script in the appropriate interpreter, such as Python.

If we run this JavaScript file (from a command-line window) we see these results in the cell output:

```
$ node Stats+Analysis.js
Raw data is  [ 98, 98.6, 98.4, 98.8, 200, 120, 98.5 ]
Standard Deviation is  35.07
Mean is  116.04
Median is  98.6
Median Abs Deviation is 0.20000000000000284
The outliers of the data set are  [ 4, 5, 6 ]
The data set without outliers is  [ 98, 98.6, 98.4, 98.8 ]
```

HTML format

The HTML (`.html`) format corresponds to the HTML needed to display the page as it appears in your notebook in a web browser. The generated HTML does not have any coding logic–it only has the HTML necessary to display a similar page.

The HTML format would be useful to convey to another user the results of your notebook. You may want to do this if you wanted to e-mail your notebook to another user (where the raw HTML would be transported and viewable in an e-mail client application).

HTML is also useful if you have a web service available where you can insert new pages. If the web server does not have support for Jupyter files (refer to the first section of this chapter), HTML may be your only choice. Similarly, you may not want to hand over your source Jupyter Notebook (IPYNB) file even if the web server does support Jupyter.

The exported HTML format looks like this in a browser:

```
In [17]:  const stats = require("stats-analysis");

          var arr = [98, 98.6, 98.4, 98.8, 200, 120, 98.5];

          //standard deviation
          var my_stddev = stats.stdev(arr).toFixed(2);

          //mean
          var my_mean = stats.mean(arr).toFixed(2);

          //median
          var my_median = stats.median(arr);

          //median absolute deviation
          var my_mad = stats.MAD(arr);

          // Outlier detection. Returns indexes of outliers
          var my_outliers = stats.indexOfOutliers(arr);

          // Remove the outliers
          var my_without_outliers = stats.filterOutliers(arr);

          //display our stats
          console.log("Raw data is ", arr);
          console.log("Standard Deviation is ", my_stddev);
          console.log("Mean is ", my_mean);
          console.log("Median is ", my_median);
          console.log("Median Abs Deviation is " + my_mad);
          console.log("The outliers of the data set are ", my_outliers);
          console.log("The data set without outliers is ", my_without_outliers);

          Raw data is  [ 98, 98.6, 98.4, 98.8, 200, 120, 98.5 ]
          Standard Deviation is  35.07
          Mean is  116.04
          Median is  98.6
          Median Abs Deviation is 0.20000000000000284
          The outliers of the data set are  [ 4, 5, 6 ]
          The data set without outliers is  [ 98, 98.6, 98.4, 98.8 ]

Out[17]:  undefined
```

Notice that none of the Jupyter heading information is displayed or available. Otherwise, it does look the same as the Jupyter display.

Markdown format

Markdown (.md) format is a looser version of HTML (remember that HTML stands for Hypertext Markup Language). MD files can be used by some tools. It is normally used as the format of README files for software distributions (where the client's capabilities for display can be very limited).

For example, the Markdown format of the same notebook is as follows:

```javascript
const stats = require("stats-analysis");
var arr = [98, 98.6, 98.4, 98.8, 200, 120, 98.5];
//standard deviation
var my_stddev = stats.stdev(arr).toFixed(2);
//mean
var my_mean = stats.mean(arr).toFixed(2);
//median
var my_median = stats.median(arr);
//median absolute deviation
var my_mad = stats.MAD(arr);
// Outlier detection. Returns indexes of outliers
var my_outliers = stats.indexOfOutliers(arr);
// Remove the outliers
var my_without_outliers = stats.filterOutliers(arr);
//display our stats
console.log("Raw data is ", arr);
...
```

Obviously, the Markdown format is a very low-level display. There are only minor text markings that help the reader determine the different formatting in use. I used the Atom editor to see what this looks like interpreted:

```
Stats+Analysis-1.rst    Stats+Analysis.md
  4    const stats = require("stats-analysis");
  5
  6    var arr = [98, 98.6, 98.4, 98.8, 200, 120, 98.5];
  7
  8    //standard deviation
  9    var my_stddev = stats.stdev(arr).toFixed(2);
 10
 11    //mean
 12    var my_mean = stats.mean(arr).toFixed(2);
 13
 14    //median
 15    var my_median = stats.median(arr);
 16
 17    //median absolute deviation
 18    var my_mad = stats.MAD(arr);
 19
 20    // Outlier detection. Returns indexes of outliers
 21    var my_outliers = stats.indexOfOutliers(arr);
 22
 23    // Remove the outliers
 24    var my_without_outliers = stats.filterOutliers(arr);
 25
 26    //display our stats
 27    console.log("Raw data is ", arr);
 28    console.log("Standard Deviation is ", my_stddev);
 29    console.log("Mean is ", my_mean);
 30    console.log("Median is ", my_median);
 31    console.log("Median Abs Deviation is " + my_mad);
 32    console.log("The outliers of the data set are ", my_outliers);
 33    console.log("The data set without outliers is ", my_without_outliers);
 34
 35
 36    ```
 37
 38        Raw data is  [ 98, 98.6, 98.4, 98.8, 200, 120, 98.5 ]
```

Again, a very clean display –still close to the Jupyter Notebook display.

reStructuredText format

The reStructuredText (.rst) format is a simple, plain-text markup language that is sometimes used for programming documentation.

For example, the RST format for the example page looks like this:

```python
.. code:: python
    const stats = require("stats-analysis");
    var arr = [98, 98.6, 98.4, 98.8, 200, 120, 98.5];
    //standard deviation
    var my_stddev = stats.stdev(arr).toFixed(2);
    //mean
    var my_mean = stats.mean(arr).toFixed(2);
    //median
    var my_median = stats.median(arr);
    //median absolute deviation
    var my_mad = stats.MAD(arr);
    // Outlier detection. Returns indexes of outliers
    var my_outliers = stats.indexOfOutliers(arr);
    // Remove the outliers
    var my_without_outliers = stats.filterOutliers(arr);
    //display our stats
    console.log("Raw data is ", arr);

...
```

As you can see, it is similar to the Markdown in the previous example–just gives a rudimentary breakout of the code into chunks.

Using Atom for display the RST file results in this:

```
Stats+Analysis-1.rst    Stats+Analysis.md
 6        var arr = [98, 98.6, 98.4, 98.8, 200, 120, 98.5];
 7
 8        //standard deviation
 9        var my_stddev = stats.stdev(arr).toFixed(2);
10
11        //mean
12        var my_mean = stats.mean(arr).toFixed(2);
13
14        //median
15        var my_median = stats.median(arr);
16
17        //median absolute deviation
18        var my_mad = stats.MAD(arr);
19
20        // Outlier detection. Returns indexes of outliers
21        var my_outliers = stats.indexOfOutliers(arr);
22
23        // Remove the outliers
24        var my_without_outliers = stats.filterOutliers(arr);
25
26        //display our stats
27        console.log("Raw data is ", arr);
28        console.log("Standard Deviation is ", my_stddev);
29        console.log("Mean is ", my_mean);
30        console.log("Median is ", my_median);
31        console.log("Median Abs Deviation is " + my_mad);
32        console.log("The outliers of the data set are ", my_outliers);
33        console.log("The data set without outliers is ", my_without_outliers);
34
35
36
37
38    .. parsed-literal::
39
40        Raw data is  [ 98, 98.6, 98.4, 98.8, 200, 120, 98.5 ]
```

The RST display is not as nice as some of the others.

PDF format

The PDF (.pdf) format is a well-known display format used for many sources. PDF is a good format for conveying unmodifiable content to other users. The other users will not be able to modify results in any way, but they will be able to see and understand your logic.

Jupyter uses the **LaTeX** package to export the image of the notebook to a PDF file. You have to install this package on your machine in order for this to work. On Mac, this involves the following:

- Install LaTex–there are separate installations for Windows and Mac
- The following (Mac) commands for fonts:

```
sudo tlmgr install adjustbox
sudo tlmgr install collection-fontsrecommended
```

 Note this installation was pretty cumbersome. I installed the full LaTeX, then another note said to install a mini version of LaTeX. And then it was tricky to install the fonts. I have very little confidence these steps will work correctly on a Windows machine.

If you do not have the full set of the packages needed, when you try to download the PDF file, a new screen will open in your notebook and a long error message will be displayed showing what piece is missing.

For our example, the generated PDF file looks like this:

Stats Analysis

July 14, 2016

```
In [17]: const stats = require("stats-analysis");

         var arr = [98, 98.6, 98.4, 98.8, 200, 120, 98.5];

         //standard deviation
         var my_stddev = stats.stdev(arr).toFixed(2);

         //mean
         var my_mean = stats.mean(arr).toFixed(2);

         //median
         var my_median = stats.median(arr);
```

I think this is a nice, clean display of your notebook.

Summary

In this chapter, we shared notebooks on a notebook server. We added a notebook to our web server. And we distributed at notebook using GitHub. We also looked into converting our notebooks into different formats, such as HTML and PDF.

In the next chapter, we will learn about overcoming problems where multiple users are accessing our notebook at the same time.

8

Multiuser Jupyter Notebooks

Jupyter notebooks have the inherent ability to be modified by users as and when the user enters data or makes a selection. However, there is an issue with the standard implementation of the notebook server software that does not account for more than one person working on a notebook at the same time. The notebook server software is the underlying Jupyter software that displays the page and interacts with the user—it follows the directions in your notebook for display and interaction.

A notebook server, really a specialized internet web server, typically creates a new path or thread of execution for each user to allow for multiple users. A problem comes up when a lower level subroutine, used for all instances, does not properly account for multiple users where each has their own set of data.

 Some of the coding/installs of this chapter may not work in a Windows environment.

In this chapter, we will do the following:

- We will give an example of the issue that occurs when multiple users access the same notebook in a standard Jupyter installation
- We will use a new version of Jupyter, JupyterHub, that was built by extending upon Jupyter to specifically address the multiple user problem
- We will also use Docker, a tool to allow for multiple instances of any software, to address the issue

Sample interactive notebook

For this chapter, we will use a simple notebook that asks the user for some information and displays other information.

For example, we could have a script such as this (taken from Chapter 7, *Sharing and Converting Jupyter Notebooks*):

```
from ipywidgets import interact
def myfunction(x):
    return x
interact(myfunction, x= "Hello World ")
```

The script presents a textbox to the user with the original value of the box containing the "Hello World" string. As the user interacts with the input field and changes the value, the value of the variable x in the script changes accordingly and is displayed on screen. For example, I have changed the value to the letter A:

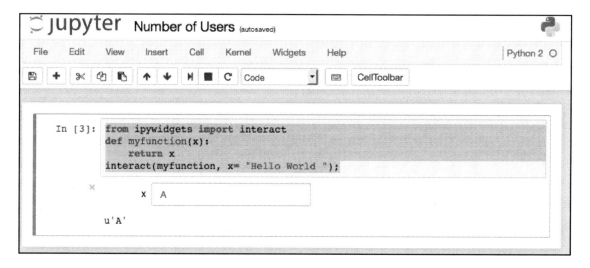

We can see the multiuser problem if we just open the same page in another browser window (copy the URL, open a new browser window, paste in the URL, and hit *Enter*)–we get the exact same display pulling up the last checkpoint. The new window should have started with a new script, just prompting you with the default "Hello World" message. However, since the Jupyter server software is only expecting one user, there is only one copy of the variable x, so it displays its value.

JupyterHub

Once Jupyter notebooks were shared, it became obvious that the multiuser problem had to be solved. A new version of the Jupyter software was developed, called JupyterHub. JupyterHub was specifically designed to handle multiple users, giving each user their own set of variables to work with. Actually, the system will give each user a whole new instance of the Jupyter software to each user–a brute force approach, but it works.

When JupyterHub starts up, it initiates a hub or controlling agent. The hub will start an instance of a listener or proxy for Jupyter requests. When the proxy gets requests for Jupyter it turns them over to the hub. If the hub decides that this is a new user, it will generate a new instance of the Jupyter server and attach all further interactions between that user and Jupyter to their own version of the server.

Installation

JupyterHub requires Python 3.3 or newer, and we will use the `pip3` Python tool to install JupyterHub. You can check the version of Python you are running by just entering `Python` on a command line; the prologue will echo out the current version:

```
Python
Python 3.6.0a4 (v3.6.0a4:017cf260936b, Aug 15 2016, 13:38:16)
[GCC 4.2.1 (Apple Inc. build 5666) (dot 3)] on darwin
Type "help", "copyright", "credits" or "license" for more information.
```

If you need to upgrade to a new version, consult the directions on `https://www.python.org/` as the directions are operating system and Python version-specific.

JupyterHub is installed much like other software, using the following commands:

```
npm install -g configurable-http-proxy
pip3 install jupyterhub
```

First, we install the proxy. The `-g` on the proxy install makes that software available to all users:

```
npm install -g configurable-http-proxy
/usr/local/bin/configurable-http-proxy ->
/usr/local/lib/node_modules/configurable-http-proxy/bin/configurable-http-proxy
    /usr/local/lib
    └─┬ configurable-http-proxy@1.3.0
      ├─┬ commander@2.9.0
      | └── graceful-readlink@1.0.1
```

```
├──┬ http-proxy@1.13.3
│  ├──── eventemitter3@1.2.0
│  └──── requires-port@1.0.0
├──┬ lynx@0.2.0
│  ├──── mersenne@0.0.3
│  └──── statsd-parser@0.0.4
├──── strftime@0.9.2
└──┬ winston@2.2.0
   ├──── async@1.0.0
   ├──── colors@1.0.3
   ├──── cycle@1.0.3
   ├──── eyes@0.1.8
   ├──── isstream@0.1.2
   ├──── pkginfo@0.3.1
   └──── stack-trace@0.0.9
```

Then we install JupyterHub:

```
pip3.6 install jupyterhub
Collecting jupyterhub
  Downloading jupyterhub-0.6.1-py3-none-any.whl (1.3MB)
    100% |████████████████████████████████| 1.4MB
789kB/s
  Collecting requests (from jupyterhub)
    Downloading requests-2.11.1-py2.py3-none-any.whl (514kB)
    100% |████████████████████████████████| 522kB
1.5MB/s
  Collecting traitlets>=4.1 (from jupyterhub)
    Downloading traitlets-4.2.2-py2.py3-none-any.whl (68kB)
    100% |████████████████████████████████| 71kB
4.3MB/s
  Collecting sqlalchemy>=1.0 (from jupyterhub)
    Downloading SQLAlchemy-1.0.14.tar.gz (4.8MB)
    100% |████████████████████████████████| 4.8MB
267kB/s
  Collecting jinja2 (from jupyterhub)
    Downloading Jinja2-2.8-py2.py3-none-any.whl (263kB)
    100% |████████████████████████████████| 266kB
838kB/s
  ...
```

Operation

We can now start JupyterHub directly from the command line:

```
jupyterhub
```

This results in the following display, which will appear in the command console window:

```
[I 2016-08-28 14:30:57.895 JupyterHub app:643] Writing cookie_secret to
/Users/dtoomey/jupyterhub_cookie_secret
    [W 2016-08-28 14:30:57.953 JupyterHub app:304]
        Generating CONFIGPROXY_AUTH_TOKEN. Restarting the Hub will require
restarting the proxy.
        Set CONFIGPROXY_AUTH_TOKEN env or JupyterHub.proxy_auth_token
config to avoid this message.
    [W 2016-08-28 14:30:57.962 JupyterHub app:757] No admin users, admin
interface will be unavailable.
    [W 2016-08-28 14:30:57.962 JupyterHub app:758] Add any administrative
users to `c.Authenticator.admin_users` in config.
    [I 2016-08-28 14:30:57.962 JupyterHub app:785] Not using whitelist. Any
authenticated user will be allowed.
    [I 2016-08-28 14:30:57.992 JupyterHub app:1231] Hub API listening on
http://127.0.0.1:8081/hub/
    [E 2016-08-28 14:30:57.998 JupyterHub app:963] Refusing to run
JuptyterHub without SSL. If you are terminating SSL in another layer, pass
--no-ssl to tell JupyterHub to allow the proxy to listen on HTTP.
```

 Notice that the script completed, and a window did not open for you in your default browser as it would in the standard Jupyter installation.

The most important feature of this is the last line of output (which is also printed on screen in red) `Refusing to run JupyterHub without SSL`. JupyterHub is specifically built to account for multiple users logging in and using a single notebook, so it is complaining that it expected to have SSL running (to secure user interactions).

The last half of the last line gives us a clue what to do–we need to tell JupyterHub that we are not using a certificate/SSL. We can do that with the `--no-ssl` argument, as follows:

```
Jupyterhub --no-ssl
```

This leads to the expected result in the console, and leaves the server still running:

```
[I 2016-08-28 14:43:15.423 JupyterHub app:622] Loading cookie_secret
from /Users/dtoomey/jupyterhub_cookie_secret
    [W 2016-08-28 14:43:15.447 JupyterHub app:304]
```

```
        Generating CONFIGPROXY_AUTH_TOKEN. Restarting the Hub will require
restarting the proxy.
        Set CONFIGPROXY_AUTH_TOKEN env or JupyterHub.proxy_auth_token
config to avoid this message.
    [W 2016-08-28 14:43:15.450 JupyterHub app:757] No admin users, admin
interface will be unavailable.
    [W 2016-08-28 14:43:15.450 JupyterHub app:758] Add any administrative
users to `c.Authenticator.admin_users` in config.
    [I 2016-08-28 14:43:15.451 JupyterHub app:785] Not using whitelist. Any
authenticated user will be allowed.
    [I 2016-08-28 14:43:15.462 JupyterHub app:1231] Hub API listening on
http://127.0.0.1:8081/hub/
    [W 2016-08-28 14:43:15.468 JupyterHub app:959] Running JupyterHub
without SSL. There better be SSL termination happening somewhere else...
    [I 2016-08-28 14:43:15.468 JupyterHub app:968] Starting proxy @
http://*:8000/
    14:43:15.867 - info: [ConfigProxy] Proxying http://*:8000 to
http://127.0.0.1:8081
    14:43:15.871 - info: [ConfigProxy] Proxy API at
http://127.0.0.1:8001/api/routes
    [I 2016-08-28 14:43:15.900 JupyterHub app:1254] JupyterHub is now
running at http://127.0.0.1:8000/
```

If we now go to that URL (`http://127.0.0.1:8000/`) shown on the last line of the output, we get to a login screen for JupyterHub:

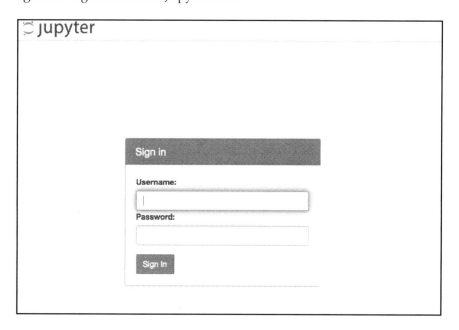

So, we have avoided requiring SSL, but we still need to configure the users for the system. Note that, not using SSL will expose aspects of the machine that you may not want.

The JupyterHub software uses a configuration file to determine how it should work. You can generate a configuration file using JupyterHub, and provide default values using the following command:

```
jupyterhub --generate-config
Writing default config to: jupyterhub_config.py
```

The file will be generated in the current directory. You need to move the file to the `jupyterhub` directory to enact your changes. The generated configuration file has close to 500 lines available. The start of the sample file is shown here:

```
# Configuration file for jupyterhub.
c = get_config()
#-----------------------------------------------------------------------
----


# JupyterHub configuration

#-----------------------------------------------------------------------
----
# An Application for starting a multiuser Jupyter Notebook server.
# JupyterHub will inherit config from: Application
# Include any kwargs to pass to the database connection. See
# sqlalchemy.create_engine for details.
# c.JupyterHub.db_kwargs = {}
# The base URL of the entire application
# c.JupyterHub.base_url = '/'
...
```

As you can see, most of the configuration settings are prefixed with a pound sign (#) denoting that they are commented out. The setting that is mentioned is the default value that will be applied. If you needed to change one of the settings you would remove the prefix sharp symbol and change the right-hand side of the equal sign (=) to your new value. By the way, this is a good way to test out changes: make one change, save the file, try out your change, and continue with any additional changes. As you progress, if one change does not work as expected, you need only to replace the pound sign and you are back to a working position.

We will look at a few of the configuration options available. It is interesting to note that many of the settings in this file are Python settings, not particular to JupyterHub. The list of items includes the following:

Area	Description
JupyterHub	Settings for JupyterHub
LoggingConfigurable	Logging information layout
SingletonConfigurable	A configurable that only allows one instance
Application	Date format and logging level
Security	SSL certificate
Spawner	How the hub starts new instances of Jupyter for new users
LocalProcessSpawner	Uses `Popen` to start local processes as users
Authenticator	The method(s) used to authenticate the user
PAMAuthenticator	Interaction with Linux to login
LocalAuthenticator	Checks for local users, and can attempt to create them if they exist

Continuing with operations

I made no changes to the configuration file to get my installation up and running. By default, the configuration uses the PEM system, which will use the user credentials manually added into the form and operating system that you are running on to pass in credentials (as if they were logging into the machine) for validation. Note that, there are cases where an SSL error occurs in this step, which will require you to rename the `./jupyter` directory.

If you are seeing the message **JupyterHub single-user server requires notebook >= 4.0** in the console log when trying to login to your JupyterHub installation, you need to update the base Jupyter using the following command:

```
pip3 install jupyter
```

This will update your base `jupyter` to the latest version, currently 4.1.

 If you do not have `pip3` installed, you need to upgrade to Python 3 or newer. See the documentation at `https://www.python.org/` for the steps for your system.

Now, you can start JupyterHub using the following command line:

```
jupyterhub --no-ssl
```

Alternatively, you may use a certificate from the previous chapter. Log in on the login screen using the same credentials you use to login to the machine (remember, JupyterHub is using PEM, which calls into your operating system to validate credentials). You will end up in something that looks very much like your standard Jupyter homepage:

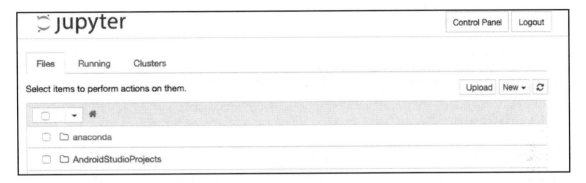

It looks very similar, except there are now two additional buttons in the top right of the screen:

- **Control Panel**
- **Logout**

Clicking on the **Logout** button logs you out of JupyterHub and redirects you to the login screen.

Clicking on the **Control Panel** button brings you to a new screen with two options, shown here:

- **Stop My Server**
- **My Server**

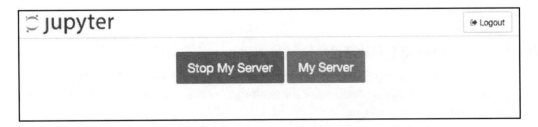

Clicking on the **Stop My Server** button stops your Jupyter installation and brings you to a page with one button: **My Server** (as shown after this section). You might also have noticed the changes that have occurred in the console log of your command line:

```
    [I 2016-08-28 20:22:16.578 JupyterHub log:100] 200 GET
/hub/api/authorizations/cookie/jupyter-hub-token-dtoomey/[secret]
(dtoomey@127.0.0.1) 13.31ms
    [I 2016-08-28 20:23:01.181 JupyterHub orm:178] Removing user dtoomey
from proxy
    [I 2016-08-28 20:23:01.186 dtoomey notebookapp:1083] Shutting down
kernels
    [I 2016-08-28 20:23:01.417 JupyterHub base:367] User dtoomey server
took 0.236 seconds to stop
    [I 2016-08-28 20:23:01.422 JupyterHub log:100] 204 DELETE
/hub/api/users/dtoomey/server (dtoomey@127.0.0.1) 243.06ms
```

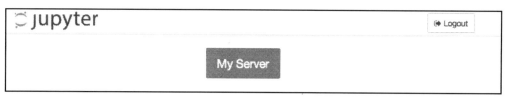

Clicking on the **My Server** button brings you back to the Jupyter home page. If you had hit the **Stop My Server** button earlier, then the underlying Jupyter software would be restarted, as you may notice in the console output (which I have shown here):

```
    I 2016-08-28 20:26:16.356 JupyterHub base:306] User dtoomey server took
1.007 seconds to start
    [I 2016-08-28 20:26:16.356 JupyterHub orm:159] Adding user dtoomey to
proxy /user/dtoomey => http://127.0.0.1:50972
    [I 2016-08-28 20:26:16.372 dtoomey log:47] 302 GET /user/dtoomey
(127.0.0.1) 0.73ms
    [I 2016-08-28 20:26:16.376 JupyterHub log:100] 302 GET
/hub/user/dtoomey (dtoomey@127.0.0.1) 1019.24ms
    [I 2016-08-28 20:26:16.413 JupyterHub log:100] 200 GET
/hub/api/authorizations/cookie/jupyter-hub-token-dtoomey/[secret]
(dtoomey@127.0.0.1) 10.75ms
```

JupyterHub summary

So, in summary, with JupyterHub we have an installation of Jupyter that will maintain a separate instance of the Jupyter software for each user, thereby avoiding any collision due to variable values. The software knows whether to instantiate a new instance of Jupyter since the user logs in to the application and the system maintains a user list.

Docker

Docker is another mechanism that can be used to allow multiple users of the same notebook without collision. Docker is a system that allows you to construct sets of applications into an *image* that can be run in a container. It runs in most environments. Docker allows for many instances of an image to be run in the same machine, but maintains separate address space, so each user of a Docker image has their own instance of the software and their own set of data/variables.

Each image is a complete stack of software necessary to run, for example, a web server, web application(s), API(s), and so on.

It is not a large leap to think of an image of your notebook. The image contains Jupyter server code and your notebook. The result is a completely intact unit that does not share any space with another's instance.

Installation

Installing Docker involves downloading the latest version (the docker.dmg file for a Mac and the EXE install for Windows) and then copying the Docker applications into your Applications folder. Older Mac editions may need to use Docker toolbox instead.

Docker QuickStart Terminal is the go-to application for most developers. Docker QuickStart will start Docker on your local machine, allocate an IP address/port for addressing the Docker application(s), and bring you into the Docker terminal. Once QuickStart has completed, if you have installed your image, you could access your application (in this case your Jupyter Notebook).

From the Docker terminal, you can load images, remove images, check status, and so on.

Starting Docker

If you run Docker Quickstart, you will be brought to the Docker terminal window with a display like this:

```
    bash --login '/Applications/Docker/Docker Quickstart
Terminal.app/Contents/Resources/Scripts/start.sh'
    Last login: Tue Aug 30 08:25:11 on ttys000
    bos-mpdc7:Applications dtoomey$ bash --login
'/Applications/Docker/Docker Quickstart
Terminal.app/Contents/Resources/Scripts/start.sh'
    Starting "default"...
```

```
(default) Check network to re-create if needed...
(default) Waiting for an IP...
Machine "default" was started.
Waiting for SSH to be available...
Detecting the provisioner...
Started machines may have new IP addresses. You may need to re-run the
`docker-machine env` command.
Regenerate TLS machine certs?  Warning: this is irreversible. (y/n):
Regenerating TLS certificates
Waiting for SSH to be available...
Detecting the provisioner...
Copying certs to the local machine directory...
Copying certs to the remote machine...
Setting Docker configuration on the remote daemon...
                        ##         .
                  ## ## ##        ==
               ## ## ## ## ##    ===
           /"""""""""""""""""""\___/ ===
      ~~~ {~~ ~~~~ ~~~ ~~~~ ~~~ ~ /  ===- ~~~
           _____ o           __/
             \    \         __/
              _____/
docker is configured to use the default machine with IP 192.168.99.100
For help getting started, check out the docs at https://docs.docker.com
```

(The odd graphic near the end of the display is a character representation of a whale–the logo for Docker.)

You can see the following from the output:

- The Docker machine was started–the Docker machine controls the images that are running in your space.

- If you are using certificates, the certificates are copied into your Docker space.
- Lastly, it tells you the IP address to use when accessing your Docker instances–it should be the IP address of the machine you are using.

Building your Jupyter image for Docker

Docker knows about images that contain the entire software stack necessary to run an application. We need to build an image with a notebook and place it in Docker.

We need to download all of the Jupyter-Docker coding necessary. In the Docker terminal window, we run the `docker pull jupyter/all-spark-notebook` command:

```
docker pull jupyter/all-spark-notebook
Using default tag: latest
latest: Pulling from jupyter/all-spark-notebook
8b87079b7a06: Pulling fs layer
872e508604af: Pulling fs layer
8e8d83eda71c: Pull complete
. . .
```

This is a large download that will take some time. It is downloading and installing all of the possibly necessary components needed to run Jupyter in an image. Remember, each image is completely self-contained, so each image has *all* of the software needed to run Jupyter.

Once the download is complete, we can start an image for our notebook using a command such as the following:

```
docker run -d -p 8888:8888 -v /disk-directory:/virtual-notebook
jupyter/all-spark-notebook
```

The parts of this command are as follows:

- `docker run`: The command to Docker to start executing an image.
- `-d`: Run the image as a server (daemon) that will continue running until manually stopped by the user.
- `-p 8888:8888`: Expose the internal port `8888` to external users with the same port address. Notebooks use port `8888` by default already, so we are saying just expose the same port.
- `-v /disk-directory:/virtual-notebook`: Take the notebook from the disk directory and expose it as the virtual notebook name.
- The last argument is to use the `all-spark-notebook` as the basis for this image.

In my case, I used the following command:

```
$ docker run -d -p 8888:8888 -v /Users/dtoomey:
/dan-notebook jupyter/all-spark-notebook
b59eaf0cae67506e4f475a9861f61c01c5af3556489992104c4ce39343e8eb02
```

The big hex number displayed is the image identifier.

We can make sure the image is running using the `docker ps -1` command, which lists out the images in our `docker`:

```
$ docker ps -1
CONTAINER ID          IMAGE                          COMMAND
CREATED               STATUS              PORTS
NAMES
b59eaf0cae67          jupyter/all-spark-notebook     "tini -- start-
notebo"    8 seconds ago       Up 7 seconds         0.0.0.0:8888-
>8888/tcp    modest_bardeen
```

The parts of the display are as follows:

- The first name, `b59eaf0cae67`, is the assigned `ID` of the container. Each image in Docker is assigned to a container.
- The `IMAGE` is `Jupyter/all-spark-notebook`–it contains all of the software needed to run your notebook.
- The command is telling Docker to start the image.
- The port access point is as we expected: `8888`.
- Lastly, Docker assigns random names to every running image; ours is `modest bardeen` (I'm not sure why they do this).

At this point, we should be able to access the notebook from an external browser at `http:// 192.168.99.100:8888`. We saw this IP address when Docker started (`192.168.99.100`), and we are using port `8888` as we specified. You can subsequently shut down the existing server:

You can see the URL in the top-left corner. Below that we have a standard empty notebook.

The Docker image used has all of the latest software, so you do not have to do anything special to get updated software or components for your notebook. You can see the language options available by pulling down the **New** menu:

We will discuss using Scala in a notebook in the next chapter.

Docker summary

We have installed Docker and created an image with our notebook. We then placed the Docker image into Docker and accessed our Docker notebook image.

Summary

In this chapter, we learned how to expose a notebook so that multiple users can use a notebook at the same time. We saw an example of the *error* occurring and installed a Jupyter server that addresses the problem. We then used Docker to alleviate the issue.

In the next chapter, we will look using Scala in a notebook.

9
Jupyter Scala

The Scala language has become very popular. It is built on top of Java, so it has full interoperability, including resorting to inline Java in your Scala code. However, the syntax is much cleaner and intuitive, reworking some of the quirks in Java.

In this chapter, we will cover the following topics:

- Installing Scala for Jupyter
- Using Scala's features

Installing the Scala kernel

There is currently no process for installing the Scala kernel in a Windows environment. I'm not sure why. I expect this to change over time.

The steps for Mac OS/X are given here (taken from `https://developer.ibm.com/hadoop/2016/05/04/install-jupyter-notebook-spark`):

1. Install GIT using this:

    ```
    yum install git
    ```

2. Copy the Scala package locally:

    ```
    git clone https://github.com/alexarchambault/jupyter-scala.git
    ```

3. Install the `sbt` build tool by running this:

    ```
    sudo yum install sbt
    ```

4. Move to the Scala package directory:

```
cd jupyter-scala
```

5. Build the package:

```
sbt cli/packArchive
```

6. To launch the Scala shell, use this command:

```
./jupyter-scala
```

7. Check the kernels installed by running this command: (you should see Scala in the list now):

```
jupyter kernelspec list
```

8. Launch the Jupyter Notebook:

```
jupyter notebook
```

9. You can now choose to use a Scala 2.11 shell.

At this point, if you start Jupyter, you will see the choice for Scala listed:

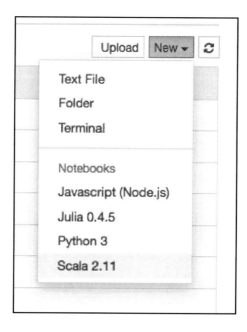

If we create a Scala notebook, we end up with the familiar layout with an icon displaying that we are running Scala and the engine type string identified as Scala 2.11:

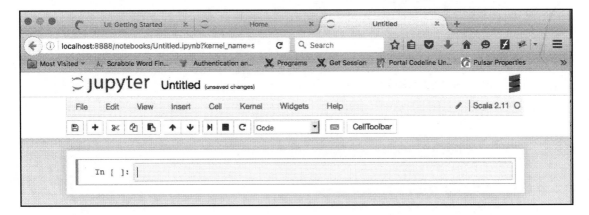

So, by naming our notebook as `Scala Notebook` and saving, we get the familiar display of notebooks on the home page, where the new notebook is called `Scala Notebook.ipynb`.

If we look in the IPYNB file, we can see the similar markup as other notebook types, with special markings for Scala:

```
{
  ...
  "metadata": {
   "kernelspec": {
    "display_name": "Scala 2.11",
    "language": "scala211",
    "name": "scala211"
   },
   "language_info": {
    "codemirror_mode": "text/x-scala",
    "file_extension": ".scala",
    "mimetype": "text/x-scala",
    "name": "scala211",
    "pygments_lexer": "scala",
    "version": "2.11.8"
   }
  ...
  }
```

Now, we can enter Scala coding into some of the cells. Following the previous language examples (from earlier chapters), we can enter this:

```
val name = "Dan"
val age = 37
show(name + " is " + age)
```

The `show` command may not work in some environments, and you can use the `print` command instead. Scala has changeable variables (`var`) and fixed variables (`val`). We are not going to be changing the fields, so they are `val` variables. The last statement, `show`, is a Jupyter extension for use in Scala to display a variable.

If we run this script in Jupyter, we see the following:

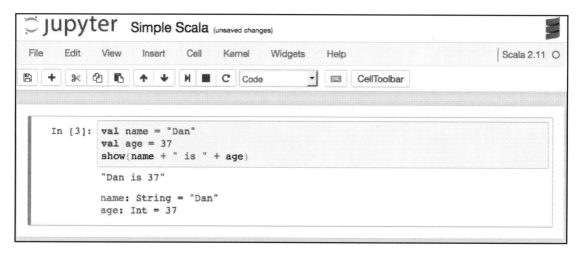

Note that, there is currently an issue connecting using Safari, connecting with Firefox works well. In the output area of the cell, we see the expected `Dan is 37`. Interestingly, Scala also displays the current type and value for each variable in the script at that point as well.

Scala data access in Jupyter

There is a copy of the iris dataset on the University of California, Irvine website at `https://archive.ics.uci.edu/ml/machine-learning-databases/iris/iris.data`. We will access this data and perform some simpler statistics on the same.

The Scala code is as follows:

```scala
import scala.io.Source;
//copied file locally https://archive.ics.uci.edu/ml/
  machine-learning-databases/iris/iris.data
val filename = "iris.data"
//DEBUGGING Uncomment this line to display more information -
println("SepalLength, SepalWidth, PetalLength, PetalWidth, Class");
val array = scala.collection.mutable.ArrayBuffer.empty[Float]
for (line <- Source.fromFile(filename).getLines) {
    var cols = line.split(",").map(_.trim);
    //println(s"${cols(0)}|${cols(1)}|${cols(2)}|
      ${cols(3)} |${cols(4)}");
    val i = cols(0).toFloat
    array += i;
}
val count = array.length;
var min:Double = 9999.0;
var max:Double = 0.0;
var total:Double = 0.0;
for ( x <- array ) {
    if (x < min) { min = x; }
    if (x > max) { max = x; }
    total += x;
}
val mean:Double = total / count;
```

Scala will complain bitterly about any excess spaces that may be in the original file. Be sure to trim the file exactly. There seems to be an issue with accessing the CSV file over the Internet. So, I copied the file locally (to the same directory where the notebook resides).

Of note in this script is that we do not have to wrap the Scala code in an object, as would normally be required since Jupyter is providing the `wrapper` class.

When we run the script, we see these results:

This is a different version of the Iris data; hence, we see different results in the statistics than we saw in `Chapter 2`, *Jupyter Python Scripting*.

Scala array operations

Scala does not have pandas, but we can emulate some of that logic with our own coding. We will use the same Titanic dataset used in Chapter 2, *Jupyter Python Scripting*, from http ://www.kaggle.com/c/titanic-gettingStarted/download/train.csv, which we have downloaded in our local space.

We can then use similar coding as was used in Chapter 2, *Jupyter Python Scripting*, on pandas:

```scala
import scala.io.Source;
val filename = "train.csv"
//PassengerId,Survived,Pclass,Name,Sex,Age,SibSp,
  Parch,Ticket,Fare,Cabin,Embarked
//1,0,3,"Braund, Mr. Owen Harris",male,22,1,0,A/5 21171,7.25,,S
var males = 0
var females = 0
var males_survived = 0
var females_survived = 0
for (line <- Source.fromFile(filename).getLines) {
    var cols = line.split(",").map(_.trim);
    var sex = cols(5);
    if (sex == "male") {
        males = males + 1;
        if (cols(1).toInt == 1) {
            males_survived = males_survived + 1;
        }
    }
    if (sex == "female") {
        females = females + 1;
        if (cols(1).toInt == 1) {
            females_survived = females_survived + 1;
        }
    }
}
val mens_survival_rate = males_survived.toFloat/males.toFloat
val womens_survival_rate = females_survived.toFloat/females.toFloat
```

In the code, we read the file line by line, parse out the columns (it is a CSV), and then make calculations based on the sex column of the data. Interestingly Scala arrays are not zero-based!

When we run this script, we see very similar results as before:

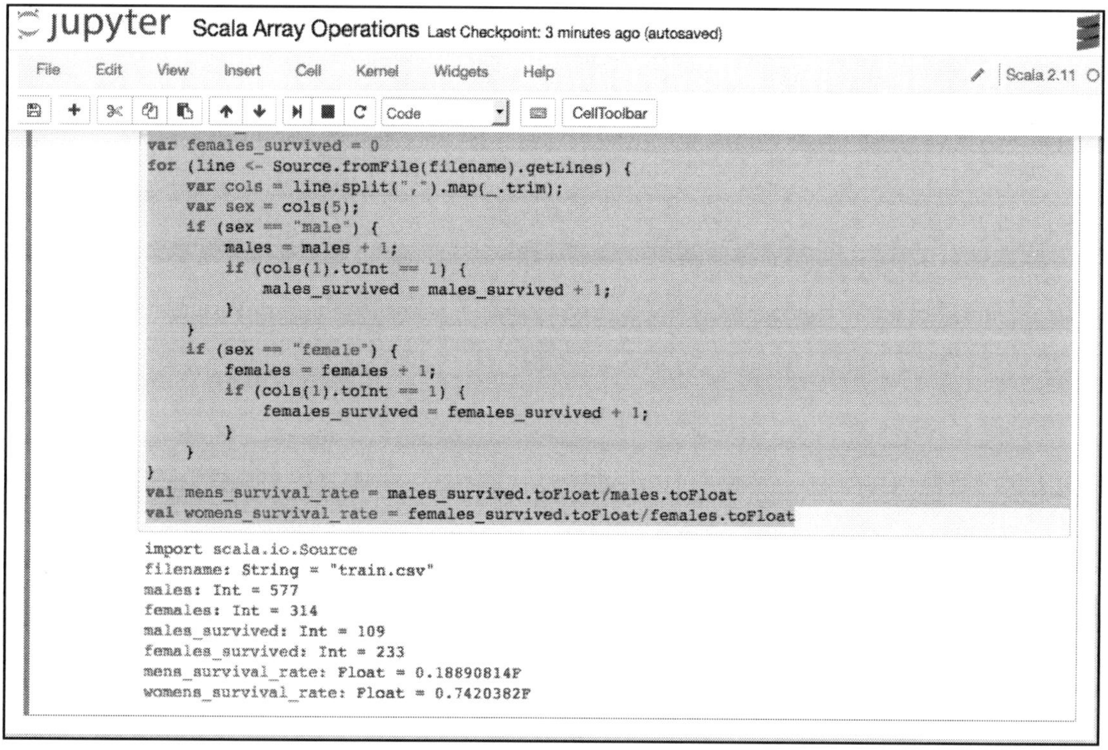

Scala random numbers in Jupyter

In this example, we simulate a rolling dice and count how many times each combination appears. We then present a simple histogram for illustrative purposes.

The script is as follows:

```
val r = new scala.util.Random
r.setSeed(113L)
val samples = 1000
var dice = new Array[Int](12)
for( i <- 1 to samples){
    var total = r.nextInt(6) + r.nextInt(6)
    dice(total) = dice(total) + 1
}
val max = dice.reduceLeft(_ max _)
for( i <- 0 to 11) {
```

```
    var str = ""
    for( j <- 1 to dice(i)/3) {
        str = str + "X"
    }
    print(i+1, str, "\n")
}
```

We first pull in the Scala random library. We set the seed (in order to have repeatable results). We are drawing 1,000 rolls. For each roll, we increment a counter of how many times the total of pips on die 1 and die 2 appear. Then we present an abbreviated histogram of the results.

Scala has a number of shortcut methods for quick scanning through a list/collection, as seen in the `reduceLeft(_ max _)` statement. We can also find the minimum value by using `min` instead of `max` in the `reduceLeft` statement.

When we run the script, we have these results:

We can see the crude histogram and the follow-on display of the current values of scalar variables in the script. Note that I divided by three so the results would fit on a page.

Scala closures

A closure is a function. The resultant function value depends on the value of the variable(s) declared outside the function.

We can use this small script to illustrate it:

```scala
var factor = 7
val multiplier = (i:Int) => i * factor
val a = multiplier(11)
val b = multiplier(12)
```

We define a function named `multiplier`. The function expects an integer argument. For each argument, we take the argument and multiply it by the external variable factor.

We see this result:

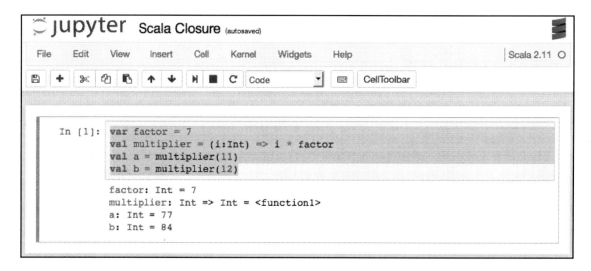

Scala higher-order functions

A higher-order function either takes other functions as arguments or returns a function as its result.

We can use this example script:

```
def squared(x: Int): Int = x * x
def cubed(x: Int): Int = x * x * x
def process(a: Int, processor: Int => Int): Int = {processor(a) }
val fiveSquared = process(5, squared)
val sevenCubed = process(7, cubed)
```

We define two functions; one squares the number passed and the other cubes the number passed.

Next, we define the higher-order function that takes the number to work on and the processor to apply.

Lastly, we call each one. For example, we call process() with 5 and the squared() function. The process() function passes the 5 to the squared() function and returns the result:

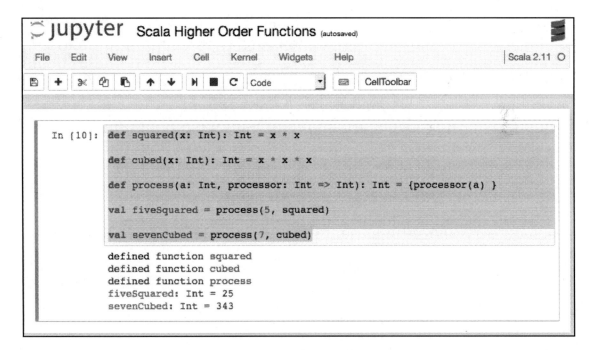

We take advantage of the Scala's engine automatically printing out variable values to see the result expected.

Scala pattern matching

Scala has very useful, built-in pattern matching. Pattern matching can be used to test for exact and/or partial matches of entire values, parts of objects, and so on; you name it!

We can use this sample script for reference:

```
def matchTest(x: Any): Any = x match {
  case 7 => "seven"
  case "two" => 2
  case _ => "something"
}
val isItTwo = matchTest("two")
val isItTest = matchTest("test")
val isItSeven = matchTest(7)
```

We define a function called `matchTest`. It takes any kind of argument and can return any type of result (not sure if that is real-life programming!).

The keyword of interest is `match`. This means the function will walk down the list of choices until it gets a match on the value x passed and then returns it.

As you can see, we have numbers and strings as input and output.

The last `case` statement is a wildcard, catchall–if the code gets that far, it will match any argument.

We can see the output here:

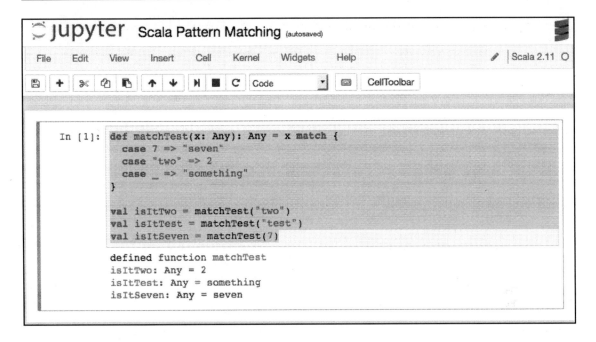

Scala case classes

A case class is a simplified type that can be used without calling out `new Classname(..)`. For example, we could have this script, which defines a case class and uses it:

```scala
case class Car(brand: String, model: String)
val buickLeSabre = Car("Buick", "LeSabre")
```

So, we have a case class called `Car`. We make an instance of that class called `buickLeSabre`.

Case classes are most useful for pattern matching since we can easily construct complex objects and examine their contents. Here's an example:

```scala
def carType(car: Car) = car match {
  case Car("Honda", "Accord") => "sedan"
  case Car("GM", "Denali") => "suv"
  case Car("Mercedes", "300") => "luxury"
  case Car("Buick", "LeSabre") => "sedan"
  case _ => "Car: is of unknown type"
}
val typeOfBuick = carType(buickLeSabre)
```

We define a pattern match block (as in the previous section of this chapter). In the match, we look at a `Car` object that has brand = GM, model = `Denali`, and so on. For each of the models of interest, we classify its type. We also have catchall at the end, so we can catch unexpected values.

We can exercise case classes in Jupyter, as shown in this screenshot:

We defined and used the `Car` case class. We then did pattern matching using the `Car` case class.

Scala immutability

Immutable means you cannot change something. In Scala, all variables are immutable unless specifically marked otherwise. This is the opposite of languages such as Java, where all variables are mutable unless specifically marked otherwise.

In Java, we can have the following function:

```
public void calculate(integer amount) {
}
```

We can modify the value of `amount` inside the `calculate` function. We can tell Java not to allow changing the value if we use the `final` keyword:

```
public void calculate(final integer amount) {
}
```

Whereas in Scala, the similar routine is as follows:

```
def calculate (amount: Int): Int = {
    amount = amount + 1;
    return amount;
}
```

The preceding code leaves the value of the `amount` variable as it was before the routine was called.

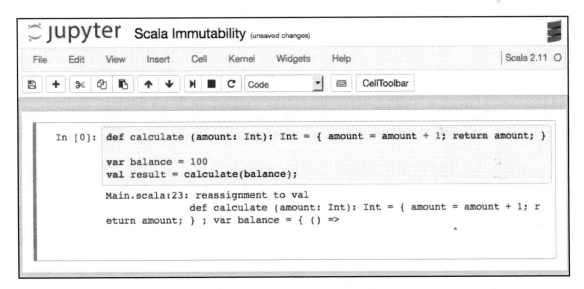

We can see in the display that even though balance is a variable (marked as `var`), Scala will not allow you to change its value inside of the function.

Scala collections

In Scala, collections are automatically mutable or immutable depending on your usage. All collections in `scala.collections.immutable` are immutable, and vice versa for `scala.collections.immutable`. Scala picks immutable collections by default, so your code will then draw automatically from the mutable collections:

```
var List mylist;
```

This happens unless you prefix your variable with `immutable`:

```
var mylist immutable.List;
```

We can see this in this small amount of code, for example:

```
var mutableList = List(1, 2, 3);
var immutableList = scala.collection.immutable.List(4, 5, 6);
mutableList.updated(1,400);
immutableList.updated(1,700);
```

As you can see in this screenshot of the notebook:

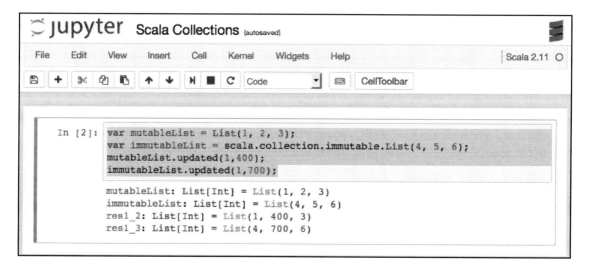

Note that Scala cheated a little here; it created a new collection when we updated `immutableList`, as you can see, with the variable name as `real_3` instead.

Named arguments

Scala allows you to specify parameter assignment by name rather than just ordinal position. For example, we can have this code:

```
def divide(dividend:Int, divisor:Int): Float =
{ dividend.toFloat / divisor.toFloat }
divide(40, 5)
divide(divisor = 40, dividend = 5)
```

If we run this in a notebook, we can see the results:

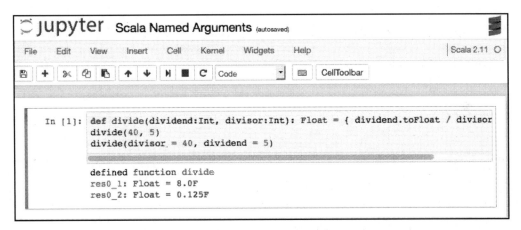

The first call is to `divide` assigned parameters by position. The second call set them accordingly.

Scala traits

A **trait** in Scala defines a set of features that can be implemented by classes. A trait is similar to an interface in Java.

A trait can be partially implemented, forcing the user (class) of the trait to implement the details.

For example, we can have this code:

```
trait Color {
    def isRed(): Boolean
}
class Red extends Color {
```

```
        def isRed() = true
    }
    class Blue extends Color {
        def isRed() = false
    }
    var red = new Red();
    var blue = new Blue();
    red.isRed()
    blue.isRed()
```

The code creates a `trait` called `Color` with one partially implemented function, `isRed`. So, every class that uses `Color` will have to implement `isRed()`.

We then implement two classes, `Red` and `Blue`, that extend the `Color` trait (this is the Scala syntax for using a trait). Since the `isRed()` function is partially implemented, both classes have to provide implementations for the `trait` function.

We can see how this operates in the following screenshot of the notebook display:

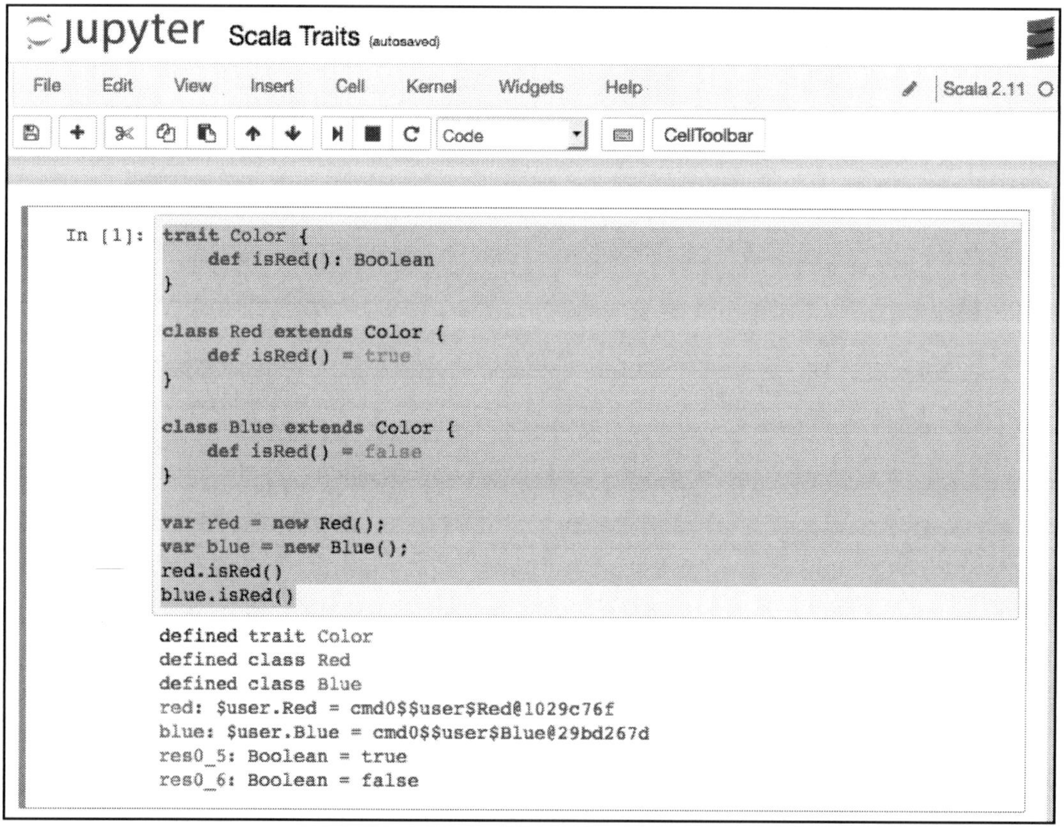

We see (in the output section at the bottom) the trait and classes created, the two instances created, and the result of calling upon the `trait` function for both classes.

Summary

In this chapter, we installed Scala for Jupyter. We used Scala coding to access data sets. We also saw how Scala can manipulate arrays. And we generated random numbers in Scala. There were examples of higher-order functions and pattern matching. We used case classes, saw examples of immutability in Scala, built collections using Scala packages, and looked at Scala traits.

In the next chapter, we will be looking at using big data in Jupyter.

10
Jupyter and Big Data

Big data is the topic on everyone's mind. I thought it would be good to see what can be done with big data in Jupyter. An up-and-coming language for dealing with large datasets is Spark. Spark is an open source big data processing framework. Spark can run over Hadoop, in the cloud, or standalone. We can use Spark coding in Jupyter much like the other languages we have seen.

In this chapter, we will cover the following topics:

- Installing Spark for use in Jupyter
- Using Spark's features

Apache Spark

One of the tools we will be using is Apache Spark. Spark is an open source toolset for cluster computing. While we will not be using a cluster, the typical usage for Spark is a larger set of machines or cluster that operate in parallel to analyze a big data set. An installation guide is available at `https://www.dataquest.io/blog/pyspark-installation-guide`. In particular, you will need to add two settings to your bash profile: `SPARK_HOME` and `PYSPARK_SUBMIT_ARGS`. `SPARK_HOME` is the directory where the software is installed. `PYSPARK_SUBMIT_ARGS` sets the number of cores to use in the local cluster.

Mac installation

To install, we download the latest TGZ file from the Spark download page at `https://spark.apache.org/downloads.html`, unpack the TGZ file, and move the unpacked directory to our Applications folder.

Spark relies on Scala's availability. We installed Scala in `Chapter 7`, *Sharing and Converting Jupyter Notebooks*.

Open a command-line window to the Spark directory and run this command:

```
brew install sbt
```

This may take a while.

Now set the configuration for Spark (for Mac) in your `.bash_profile` file:

```
# location of spark code
export SPARK_HOME="/Applications/spark-2.0.0-bin-hadoop2.7"
# machine to run on
export SPARK_MASTER_IP=127.0.0.1
export SPARK_LOCAL_IP=127.0.0.1
# python location
export PYTHONPATH=$SPARK_HOME/python/:$PYTHONPATH
export PYTHONPATH=$SPARK_HOME/python/lib/py4j-0.10.1-
src.zip:$PYTHONPATH
```

Note that, the paths used will correspond to your installation

You should now be able to run this command (from inside your Spark directory), successfully opening a command-line window in Spark:

```
bin/pyspark
```

It looks something like this (depending on the version):

```
Welcome to
```

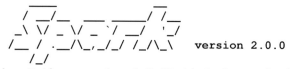

```
      ____              __
     / __/__  ___ _____/ /__
    _\ \/ _ \/ _ `/ __/  '_/
   /__ / .__/\_,_/_/ /_/\_\   version 2.0.0
      /_/
Using Python version 2.7.12 (default, Jul  2 2016 17:43:17)
SparkSession available as 'spark'.
>>>
```

You can enter `quit()` to exit.

Now, when we run our notebook, when using a Python kernel, we can access Spark.

Windows installation

We have already installed Python as part of the Jupyter installation much earlier in this book. We need to download and install the latest Spark version from `http://spark.apache.org/downloads.html`. Unpack the TGZ file and move the resulting directory to the `C:\spark directory`.

You will need to have `winutils.exe` available as well (this seems to be a problem with the Hadoop installation, but it may get fixed at some time). Download the file from `http://public-repo-1.hortonworks.com/hdp-win-alpha/winutils.exe`and install at `C:\winutils\bin`.

Now need to set up environment variables for all of these:

```
HADOOP_HOME=C:\winutils
SPARK_HOME=C:\spark
PYSPARK_DRIVER_PYTHON=ipython
PYSPARK_DRIVER_PYTHON_OPTS=notebook
```

You can start Jupyter using the `pyspark` command. You should not notice anything different about your notebook.

 We are using the Python script to invoke Spark functionality, so the language format needs to conform to Python.

Our first Spark script

Our first script reads in a text file and sees how much the line lengths add up to:

```
import pyspark
if not 'sc' in globals():
    sc = pyspark.SparkContext()
lines = sc.textFile("Spark File Words.ipynb")
lineLengths = lines.map(lambda s: len(s))
totalLength = lineLengths.reduce(lambda a, b: a + b)
print(totalLength)
```

In the script, we are first initializing Spark–only if we have not done already. Spark will complain if you try to initialize it more than once, so all Spark scripts should have this `if` prefix statement.

The script reads in a text file (the source of this script), takes every line, and computes its length; then it adds all the lengths together.

A `lambda` function is an anonymous (not named) function that takes arguments and returns a value. In the first case, given a string `s`, it returns its length.

A `reduce` function takes an argument, applies the second argument to it, replaces the first value with the result, and then proceeds with the rest of the list. In our case, it walks through the line lengths and adds them all up.

Then, running this in a notebook, we see the following result:

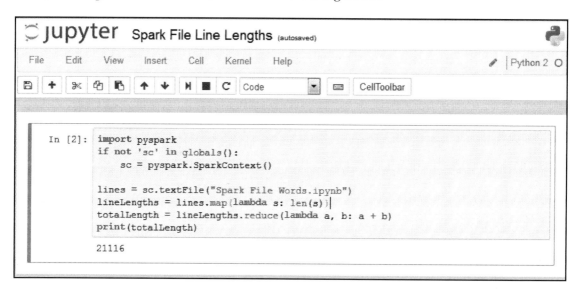

Note that the size of the file for you may be slightly different. Also, the first time you begin the Spark engine (using the `sc = pyspark.SparkContext()` line), it may take a while and your script may not complete successfully. If that happens, just try it again.

Spark word count

Now that we have seen some of the functionality, let's explore further. We can use a similar script to count the word occurrences in a file, as follows:

```python
import pyspark
if not 'sc' in globals():
    sc = pyspark.SparkContext()
text_file = sc.textFile("Spark File Words.ipynb")
counts = text_file.flatMap(lambda line: line.split(" ")) \
            .map(lambda word: (word, 1)) \
            .reduceByKey(lambda a, b: a + b)
for x in counts.collect():
    print x
```

We have the same preamble to the coding. Then we load the text file into memory.

Once the file is loaded, we split each line into words. Use a `lambda` function to tick off each occurrence of a word. The code is truly creating a new record for each word occurrence. If a word appears in the stream, a record with the count of 1 is added for that word and for every other instance the word appears, new records with the same count of 1 are added. The idea is that this process could be split over multiple processors, where each processor generates these low-level information bits. We are not concerned with optimizing this process at all.

Once we have all of these records, we reduce/summarize the record set according to the word occurrences mentioned.

The `counts` object is called a **Resilient Distributed Dataset (RDD)** in Spark. It is resilient as care is taken to persist the dataset. The RDD is distributed as it can be manipulated by all nodes in the operating cluster. And of course, it is a dataset consisting of a variety of data items.

The last `for` loop runs a `collect()` against the RDD. As mentioned, this RDD could be distributed amongst many nodes. The `collect()` function pulls all copies of the RDD into one location. Then we loop through each record.

When we run this in Jupyter, we see something akin to this display:

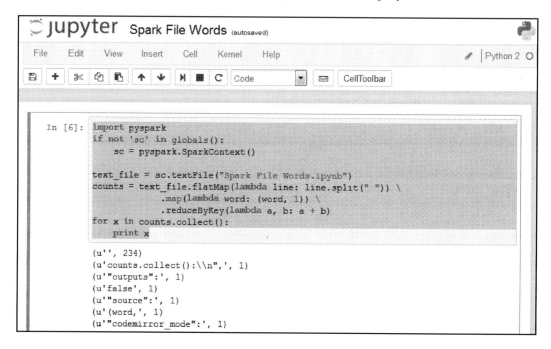

The listing is abbreviated as the list of words continues for some time. Curiously, the word splitting logic in Spark does not appear to work very well! Some of the results are not words, such as the first entry–the empty string.

Sorted word count

Using the same script with a slight modification, we can make one more call and have sorted results. The script now looks like this:

```
import pyspark
if not 'sc' in globals():
    sc = pyspark.SparkContext()
text_file = sc.textFile("Spark File Words.ipynb")
sorted_counts = text_file.flatMap(lambda line: line.split(" ")) \
            .map(lambda word: (word, 1)) \
            .reduceByKey(lambda a, b: a + b) \
            .sortByKey()
for x in sorted_counts.collect():
    print x
```

Here, we have added another function call to the RDD creation, `sortByKey()`. So, after we have map/reduced and arrived at list of words and occurrence, we can easily sort the results.

The resultant output looks like this:

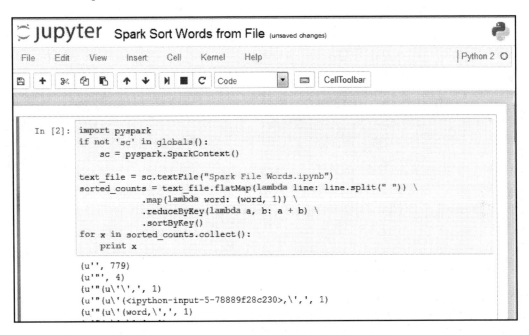

Estimate Pi

We can use map/reduce to estimate the Pi. Suppose we have code like this:

```python
import pyspark
import random
if not 'sc' in globals():
    sc = pyspark.SparkContext()
NUM_SAMPLES = 1000
def sample(p):
    x,y = random.random(),random.random()
    return 1 if x*x + y*y < 1 else 0
count = sc.parallelize(xrange(0, NUM_SAMPLES)) \
            .map(sample) \
            .reduce(lambda a, b: a + b)
print "Pi is roughly %f" % (4.0 * count / NUM_SAMPLES)
```

This code has the same preamble. We are using the `random` Python package. There is a constant for the number of samples to attempt.

We are building an RDD called `count`. We call upon the `parallelize` function to split up this process over the nodes available. The code just maps the result of the `sample` function call. Finally, we reduce the generated map set by adding all the samples.

The `sample` function gets two random numbers and returns a 1 or a 0 depending on where the two numbers end up in size. We are looking for random numbers in a small range and then comparing whether they occur within a circle of the same diameter. With a large enough sample, we would end up with Pi (3.141...).

If we run this in Jupyter, we see the following:

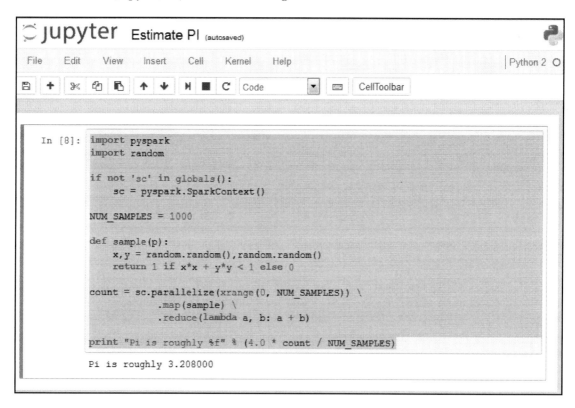

When I ran this with NUM_SAMPLES = 10000, I ended up with this:

```
PI = 3.138000.
```

Log file examination

I downloaded one of the `access_log` files from `http://www.monitorware.com/`. Like any other web access log, we have one line per entry, like this:

```
64.242.88.10 - - [07/Mar/2004:16:05:49 -0800] "GET
/twiki/bin/edit/Main/Double_bounce_sender?topicparent=Main.ConfigurationVar
iables HTTP/1.1" 401 12846
```

- The first part is the IP address of the caller, followed by timestamp, type of HTTP access, URL referenced, HTTP type, resultant HTTP Response code, and finally, the number of bytes in the response.
- We can use Spark to load in and parse out some statistics of the log entries, as in this script:

```python
import pyspark
if not 'sc' in globals():
    sc = pyspark.SparkContext()
textFile = sc.textFile("access_log")
print(textFile.count(),"access records")
gets = textFile.filter(lambda line: "GET" in line)
print(gets.count(),"GETs")
posts = textFile.filter(lambda line: "POST" in line)
print(posts.count(),"POSTs")
other = textFile.subtract(gets).subtract(posts)
print(other.count(),"Other")
for x in other.collect():
    print x
```

This script has the same preamble as others.

We read in the `access_log` file. Then we print the count of records.

Similarly, we find out how many log entries were GET and POST operations. GET is assumed to be the most prevalent.

When I first did this, I really didn't expect anything else, so I removed the `gets` and the `posts` from the set and printed out the outliers to see what they were.

When we run this in Jupyter, we see the expected output:

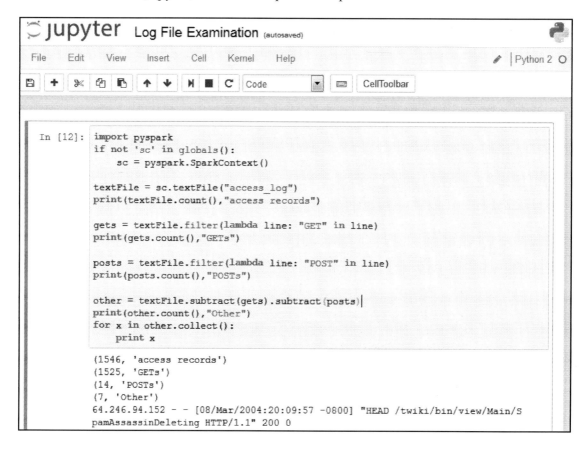

The text processing was not very fast (especially for so few records).

I liked being able to work with the data frames in such a way. There is something pleasing about being able to do basic algebra with sets in a programmatic way without having to be concerned about edge cases.

By the way, a HEAD request works just like a GET but does not return the HTTP body. This allows a caller to determine what kind of response would have come back and respond appropriately.

Spark primes

We can run a series of numbers through a filter to determine whether each number is prime or not. We can use this script:

```
import pyspark
if not 'sc' in globals():
    sc = pyspark.SparkContext()
def is_it_prime(number):
    # make sure n is a positive integer
    number = abs(int(number))
    # simple tests
    if number < 2:
        return False
    # 2 is prime
    if number == 2:
        return True
    # other even numbers aren't
    if not number & 1:
        return False
    # check whether number is divisible into it's square root
    for x in range(3, int(number**0.5)+1, 2):
        if number % x == 0:
            return False
    #if we get this far we are good
    return True
# create a set of numbers to 100,000
numbers = sc.parallelize(xrange(100000))
# count out the number of primes we found
print numbers.filter(is_it_prime).count()
```

The script generates numbers up to 100,000.

We then loop over each of the numbers and pass it to our filter. If the filter returns true, we get a record. Then we just count how many results we found.

Running this in Jupyter, we see the following:

```
number = abs(int(number))

# simple tests
if number < 2:
    return False

# 2 is prime
if number == 2:
    return True
# other even numbers aren't
if not number & 1:
    return False

# check whether number is divisible into it's square root
for x in range(3, int(number**0.5)+1, 2):
    if number % x == 0:
        return False

#if we get this far we are good
return True

# create a set of numbers to 100,000
numbers = sc.parallelize(xrange(100000))

# count out the number of primes we found
print numbers.filter(is_it_prime).count()
```
```
9592
```

This was very fast. I was waiting and didn't notice that it happened so quickly.

Spark text file analysis

In this example, we will look through a news article to determine some basic information from it.

We will be using the following script against the 2600raid news article (from `http://newsi tem.com/`):

```
import pyspark
if not 'sc' in globals():
    sc = pyspark.SparkContext()
sentences = sc.textFile('2600raid.txt') \
    .glom() \
    .map(lambda x: " ".join(x)) \
    .flatMap(lambda x: x.split("."))
print(sentences.count(),"sentences")
bigrams = sentences.map(lambda x:x.split()) \
    .flatMap(lambda x: [((x[i],x[i+1]),1) for i in range(0,len(x)-1)])
print(bigrams.count(),"bigrams")
frequent_bigrams = bigrams.reduceByKey(lambda x,y:x+y) \
    .map(lambda x:(x[1],x[0])) \
    .sortByKey(False)
frequent_bigrams.take(10)
```

The code reads in the article and splits up the article into sentences as determined by ending with a period. From there, the code maps out the bigrams present. A bigram is a pair of words that appear next to each other. We then sort the list and print out the top 10 most prevalent pairs.

When we run this in a notebook, we see these results:

```
In [11]: import pyspark

         if not 'sc' in globals():
             sc = pyspark.SparkContext()

         sentences = sc.textFile('2600raid.txt') \
             .glom() \
             .map(lambda x: " ".join(x)) \
             .flatMap(lambda x: x.split("."))
         print(sentences.count(),"sentences")

         bigrams = sentences.map(lambda x:x.split()) \
             .flatMap(lambda x: [((x[i],x[i+1]),1) for i in range(0,len(x)-1)])
         print(bigrams.count(),"bigrams")

         frequent_bigrams = bigrams.reduceByKey(lambda x,y:x+y) \
             .map(lambda x:(x[1],x[0])) \
             .sortByKey(False)
         frequent_bigrams.take(10)

         (220, 'sentences')
         (3463, 'bigrams')
Out[11]: [(36, (u'of', u'the')),
          (15, (u'the', u'mall')),
          (12, (u'At', u'this')),
          (12, (u'on', u'the')),
          (12, (u'to', u'the')),
          (11, (u'the', u'guards')),
```

I really had no idea what to expect from the output. It's curious that you can glean some insights into the article as 'the' and 'mall' appear 15 times and 'the' and 'guards' appear 11 times–a raid must have occurred in a mall and included the security guards in some manner!

Spark – evaluating history data

In this example, we combine the previous sections to look at some historical data and determine some useful attributes.

The historical data we are using is the guest list for *The Jon Stewart Show*. A typical record from the data looks like this:

```
1999,actor,1/11/99,Acting,Michael J. Fox
```

It contains the year, occupation of the guest, date of appearance, logical grouping of the occupation, and the name of the guest.

For our analysis, we will be looking at number of appearances per year, the most appearing occupation, and the most appearing personality.

We will be using this script:

```python
import pyspark
import csv
import operator
import itertools
import collections
if not 'sc' in globals():
    sc = pyspark.SparkContext()
years = {}
occupations = {}
guests = {}
#The file header contains these column descriptors
#YEAR,GoogleKnowlege_Occupation,Show,Group,Raw_Guest_List
with open('daily_show_guests.csv', 'rb') as csvfile:
    reader = csv.DictReader(csvfile)
    for row in reader:
        year = row['YEAR']
        if years.has_key(year):
            years[year] = years[year] + 1
        else:
            years[year] = 1
        occupation = row['GoogleKnowlege_Occupation']
        if occupations.has_key(occupation):
            occupations[occupation] = occupations[occupation] + 1
        else:
            occupations[occupation] = 1
        guest = row['Raw_Guest_List']
        if guests.has_key(guest):
            guests[guest] = guests[guest] + 1
        else:
```

```
                    guests[guest] = 1
    syears = sorted(years.items(), key=operator.itemgetter(1),
reverse=True)
    soccupations = sorted(occupations.items(), key=operator.itemgetter(1),
reverse=True)
    sguests = sorted(guests.items(), key=operator.itemgetter(1),
reverse=True)
    print syears[:5]
    print soccupations[:5]
    print sguests[:5]
```

The script has a number of features:

- We are using several packages.
- It has the familiar context preamble.
- We start dictionaries for the years, occupations, and guests. A dictionary contains a key and a value. For this use, the key will be the raw value from the CSV. The value will be the number of occurrences in the dataset.
- We open the file and start reading line by line using a reader object.
- On each line, we take the value of interest (`years`, `occupations`, `guests`):
  - See whether the value is present in the appropriate dictionary
  - If it is there, increment the value (counter)
  - Otherwise, initialize an entry in the dictionary
  - We then sort each of the dictionaries in reverse order of the number of appearances of the item
  - Finally, we display the top five values for each dictionary

If we run this in a notebook, we have an output like this:

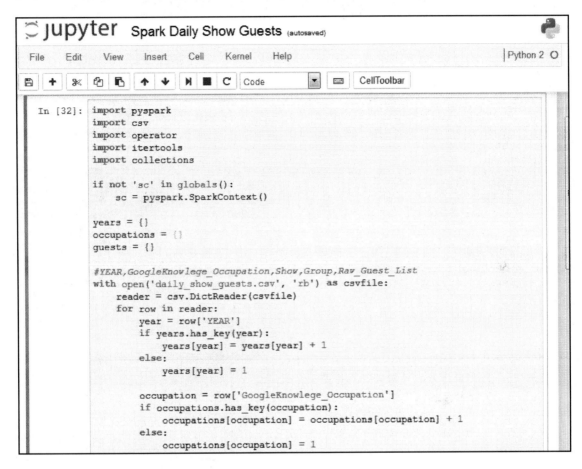

We have the first part of our script down to handling the years and occupation accumulators. Here is the rest of the script:

```
        guest = row['Raw_Guest_List']
        if guests.has_key(guest):
            guests[guest] = guests[guest] + 1
        else:
            guests[guest] = 1

syears = sorted(years.items(), key=operator.itemgetter(1), reverse=True)
soccupations = sorted(occupations.items(), key=operator.itemgetter(1), reverse=
sguests = sorted(guests.items(), key=operator.itemgetter(1), reverse=True)

print syears[:5]
print soccupations[:5]
print sguests[:5]
```

```
[('2000', 169), ('1999', 166), ('2003', 166), ('2013', 166), ('2010', 165)]
[('actor', 596), ('actress', 271), ('journalist', 180), ('author', 102), ('
Journalist', 72)]
[('Fareed Zakaria', 19), ('Denis Leary', 17), ('Brian Williams', 16), ('Pau
l Rudd', 13), ('Ricky Gervais', 13)]
```

There may be a smarter way to do all of this, but I am not aware of it! The build-up of the accumulators is pretty standard, regardless of what language you are using. I think there is an opportunity to use a map() function here. We could add each collection to the Spark Context as lists and then apply map.distinct.count.

I really liked just trimming off the lists/arrays so easily instead of having to call some function. The number of guests per year is very consistent. Actors are prevalent–probably the people of most interest to the audience. The guest list was a little surprising. The guests are mostly actors, but I think all have strong political direction.

Summary

In this chapter, we used Spark functionality via Python coding for Jupyter. First, we installed the Spark additions to Jupyter on a Windows machine and a Mac machine. We wrote an initial script that just read lines from a text file. We went further and determined the word counts in that file. We added sorting to the results. There was a script to estimate Pi. We evaluated web log files for anomalies. We determined a set of prime numbers. And we evaluated a text stream for some characteristics.

Index

Made in the USA
Middletown, DE
25 April 2018